Affirmed

Acknowledgments

First, I want to give honor and praise to God, who is my rock, my salvation, my fortress, and my shield. You have hidden me beneath your wing. I have found shelter and refuge under your shadow. You have protected me, comforted me, and cared for me. You have kept me. You breathed new life into me when I thought all hope was gone. For that, I am eternally grateful.

To my husband, Russell M. Williamson, I thank you. When I found it impossible to stand on my own, you stood with me. Truly, we have borne one another's burdens. We have held one another together through trying times and, together, have proclaimed the goodness and faithfulness of God. You have given me so many reasons to rejoice. I love you.

To my amazing children, Russ Jr., Lauren, and Courtney, and to my dear grandbaby, Leah, you all are truly a prize from God. I look at you and am constantly encouraged to be the best me possible. You are my heart's joy. You are my why. I love you with everything in me.

To my parents, Benjamin and Gretta Polote Sr., I honor you always. Your unconditional love never fails. You have taught me so much. Your words, lessons, and encouragement have carried me through many dark hours into brighter days. I thank you and I love you.

To my siblings and the rest of my family, immediate and extended, what a joy it is to be surrounded by so much love

1

and know that people genuinely care. Thank you for your love, encouragement, and support. You are very much appreciated.

To the truest friends a person can have—you know who you are. I love you! Thank you for praying for me, lifting me, loving me, believing in me, and supporting me. You have redefined the meaning of friendship for me, and I could not be more thankful.

A special thank you to Alexandria L. Barlowe, the Polote, Williamson, and Green families, and the beautiful ladies of the award-winning Blessings, Business, and Collaborations Facebook group. I love you all!

To the Reader

Affirmed is a yearlong journey with positive words, thoughts, and sayings for each day of this year. God has blessed me with the opportunity to meet and speak to hundreds of people through my coaching calls, public speaking engagements, and networking events. One of the most common themes I see in coaching and mentoring others is a lack of self-esteem, specifically dealing with negative thoughts. I began to pray for the people who told me their stories of poor self-image and lack of confidence. As I prayed, God began to give me positive words to speak to others. He gave me *Affirmed*.

God wants you to know that he loves you. He thinks the world of you. So much so that he gave his only begotten son for you. John 3:16 says, "For God so loved the world, that he gave his only begotten Son, that whosoever believes in him should not perish, but have everlasting life" (KJV2000). God does not want you to walk through life feeling less than. You will find the central theme of this book in the scripture Jeremiah 29:11 (NIV): "For I know the plans I have for you," declares the Lord, "plans to prosper you and not to harm you, plans to give you hope and a future." When you read and dwell on this scripture, you will begin to realize that there is no room for negativity in God's plan for your life. Believing this will change your mindset in a great way.

He created you in his image and he wants you to flourish and be the best version of you. I pray that as you take this yearlong journey, you realize that negative thoughts and words do not come from God. I pray that you concern yourself with God's opinion of you, not what people say or think about you. As you read, take some time to write notes in the lined sections under each affirmation. I pray that you emerge from this journey just as God intended for you to— affirmed.

January

I will forgive myself for my past mistakes.

PSALM 23:3 (NASB)
He restores my soul; He guides me in the paths
of righteousness for His name's sake.

What are you holding on to from your past?
What are you still beating yourself up about?
What situation do you continue to relive?
God has forgiven you. Now it is time for you to forgive
yourself. Today, walk in forgiveness and let go of the
guilt you have been carrying. God said that you are no
longer that person. You are no longer in that situation,
and the key to moving forward is forgiving yourself.

_____

_____

_____

_____

_____

_____

_____

I will no longer live as a victim.

1 CORINTHIANS 15:56-57 (NKJV)
The sting of death is sin, and the strength of sin
is the law. But thanks be to God, who gives us
the victory through our Lord Jesus Christ.

What situation in your life has left you feeling
like a victim? What has been said or done to you
that caused you to feel weak and powerless?
As children of God, we are victors—not victims! Do not
accept defeat in any way, shape, or form. You are not weak.
You are not powerless. Believe what God's word says
about you and about your life. Walk in your victory today.

_____

_____

_____

_____

_____

_____

_____

JANUARY 3

I will invest in personal development.

JAMES 1:5 (NKJV)
If any of you lacks wisdom, let him ask of
God, who gives to all liberally and without
reproach, and it will be given to him.

What skill have you been wanting to sharpen?
What have you said you will improve this year?
The time is now! Not later today. Not tomorrow.
Certainly not next week! The time is now. Enroll in
that class. Purchase a ticket to that seminar. Meet with
that investor. We have to stop waiting for the "perfect"
time to act on the things that will improve us. How
will you invest in your personal development today?

_____

_____

_____

_____

_____

_____

I will spend quality time with myself.

EPHESIANS 5:29 (ESV)
For no one ever hated his own flesh, but nourishes it
and cherishes it, just as Christ does the church.

When is the last time you had alone time? What
are your favorite solo activities? I challenge you
to make time to spend with yourself today. Do
something that you enjoy in your own company!

_____

_____

_____

_____

_____

_____

_____

_____

_____

I am at peace with my past.

ISAIAH 26:3 (NIV)
You will keep in perfect peace those whose minds
are steadfast, because they trust in you.

What situation from your past still causes you to be
sad? What painful memories seem to haunt you?
What is in the past belongs there. Accept the things from
your past that have hurt you. In doing so, you will free
yourself from old wounds and thus open the possibility
for new things in your life. Ask God to give you his
peace today. Stay focused on him and not your past.

_____

_____

_____

_____

_____

_____

_____

I will stop blaming people for my poor choices.

ROMANS 14:12
So then, each of us will give an account of ourselves to God.

Is there something that you have blamed on a friend
or family member that is actually your fault?
Contrary to how you may feel or what you may think,
there is great power in taking responsibility for your
choices. When you take responsibility for your choices and
actions, you are able to course correct when necessary.
What do you need to start taking responsibility for?

_____

_____

_____

_____

_____

_____

_____

_____

I deserve to be treated well.

PROVERBS 19:8 (NLT)
To acquire wisdom is to love oneself; people
who cherish understanding will prosper.

How have you been treating yourself lately? Have
you been allowing yourself to be mistreated?
When you care for and have the proper love for yourself,
you exude that to others. The same principle applies if
you do not love and care for yourself. Know that God
loves you and he wants you to love yourself. Do not
accept mistreatment in any way from anyone. Realize
that God wants the best for you, which includes wanting
you to be treated well by others. Show people how to
treat you by example, by how you treat yourself.

_____

_____

_____

_____

_____

_____

I am wonderfully made.

PSALM 129:13-14 (NIV)
For you created my inmost being; you knit me
together in my mother's womb. I praise you
because I am fearfully and wonderfully made; your
works are wonderful, I know that full well.

Have you thanked God for the systems
that make up your body lately?
When you think about the process of how our bodies
were created and all that goes into the systems that keep
us alive, you will understand that you are wonderfully
made. From our respiratory systems to our lymph
nodes, God put a great deal of time and thought into
creating us. Wiggle your fingers and toes. Take a deep
breath. Put your hand over your heart and feel the
rhythm of your heartbeat. These systems did not form
coincidentally or on accident. They are God's handiwork
and craftsmanship. What a mighty God he is!

_____

_____

_____

_____

I am brilliant.

PROVERBS 1:7
The fear of the Lord is the beginning of knowledge,
but fools despise wisdom and instruction.

God has given you a brilliant mind. He has carefully
created and crafted you in your mother's womb and
has great things for you to do in his name. Accept and
embrace this and seek out the purpose he has for your
life. How will you glorify him with your brilliance today?

_____

_____

_____

_____

_____

_____

_____

_____

_____

_____

JANUARY 10

I will smile at everyone I see today.

2 CORINTHIANS 6:6
In purity, understanding, patience and kindness;
in the Holy Spirit and in sincere love.

What does it cost you to show someone the love of God?
Have you ever noticed that someone with a bad attitude
seems to drag down the mood of the people around
them? The same can be said of someone with a good
attitude. Be that person with a good attitude. You will be
surprised at the positive impact that one smile can have!

_____

_____

_____

_____

_____

_____

_____

_____

_____

I am beautiful.

GENESIS 1:27
So God created mankind in his own image, in the image of
God he created them; male and female he created them.

Do you see yourself through God's eyes?
It's hard to have a negative view of yourself in any respect
when you think about the fact that you were made in his
image, isn't it? I challenge you to embrace the fact that
God made you just the way you are. Realize that when
God sees you, he sees you as beautiful and nothing less.

_____

_____

_____

_____

_____

_____

_____

_____

I am worth saving.

JOHN 3:16
For God so loved the world that he gave his
one and only Son, that whoever believes in
him shall not perish but have eternal life.

When God allowed Jesus to die on the cross for our
sins, he showed us just how much he loves us and just
how much we mean to him. God wants you to know
how he feels about you. It was not easy for him to
sacrifice his son, but YOU were and still are worth it!

_____

_____

_____

_____

_____

_____

_____

_____

I will not say "yes" when I mean "no."

PHILIPPIANS 4:13 (KJV2000)
I can do all things through Christ who strengthens me.

This is perhaps one of the most quoted scriptures that we hear. How many times do we over-commit ourselves to the point of being stressed out? God can strengthen us to do all things, but it is important for us to know how much is too much when it comes to committing ourselves. Know your limits and know when to say yes and when to say no.

I am worth waiting for.

GALATIANS 2:20 (ESV)
I have been crucified with Christ. It is no longer I
who live, but Christ who lives in me. And the life
I now live in the flesh I live by faith in the Son of
God, who loved me and gave himself for me.

When we fully accept and embrace who we are in Christ,
we realize that we are truly awesome in his eyes. Know
that God loves you—if you were worth the sacrifice of his
only begotten son, then surely you are worth waiting for.

I will open all of my gifts.

PROVERBS 18:16
A man's gift makes room for him and
brings him before the great.

What talents and gifts are going unused in your life? What
skill are you sitting on? God blessed you with those gifts
and talents to be a blessing to others. I challenge you to
find a way to use your talents to bless someone today.

_____

_____

_____

_____

_____

_____

_____

_____

_____

I will be mindful of the company I keep.

1 CORINTHIANS 15:33 (NASB)
Do not be deceived: "Bad company corrupts good morals."

We've all heard the old adage "one bad apple spoils
the bunch." It's true! Would you believe me if I told
you that you are essentially a culmination of the
five people you spend the most time with? Are they
people you want to be like? If the answer is no, it is
time to reevaluate your relationships with them.

I will stop procrastinating.

ECCLESIASTES 11:4 (NIV)
Whoever watches the wind will not plant;
whoever looks at the clouds will not reap.

When we delay doing things, we create unnecessary stress in our lives. This is especially true when we procrastinate in doing the things that God has instructed us to do. What has God placed on your heart to say or do? What is holding you back from doing it today? I challenge you to remove the roadblocks that are keeping you from action. Act on it now!

_____

_____

_____

_____

_____

_____

_____

I will take better care of my physical health.

1 CORINTHIANS 6:19
Do you not know that our bodies are temples of
the Holy Spirit, who is in you, whom you have
received from God? You are not your own.

When we take care of our bodies, we improve the overall
quality of our lives. We feel better, we think better, we
sleep better. Are you feeling tired and sluggish lately?
Not sleeping well? Make a few changes in your daily
choices, starting with drinking more water. Next,
make a habit of incorporating more exercise into your
daily routine. You will see and feel a difference!

I will live intentionally.

2 PETER 1:10
Therefore, my brothers and sisters, make every
effort to confirm your calling and election. For if
you do these things, you will never stumble.

How often do you feel as if you are wandering through life
without direction? God wants you to turn to him to reveal
the path that you are supposed to take. Make today the day
that you decide to start living with purpose on purpose!

_____

_____

_____

_____

_____

_____

_____

_____

_____

I will pay it forward.

HEBREWS 13:2 (NASB)
Do not neglect to show hospitality to strangers, for by
this some have entertained angels without knowing it.

Can you remember the last time you did something nice
for a total stranger? How did that make you feel? There
is nothing more heartwarming than seeing a look of
gratitude on someone's face after you have been a blessing
to them. Random acts of kindness not only bless the
recipient; they bless the giver as well. I challenge you to
find three ways to be a blessing to a total stranger today.

I will be a good steward of my resources.

MATTHEW 25:23 (NIV)
His master replied, "Well done, good and faithful servant! You have been faithful with a few things; I will put you in charge of many things. Come and share your master's happiness!"

When we are responsible with little, we show God that we can be trusted with more and vice versa. Are you managing your resources well? If the answer is no, make a change today. Find a way to make smarter financial decisions and watch God bless your efforts.

_____

_____

_____

_____

_____

_____

_____

I will stop judging people.

JOHN 8:7

When they kept on questioning him, he straightened up and said to them, "Let any one of you who is without sin be the first to throw the first stone."

Have you been highly critical of someone you know? It's easy to judge someone's situation from a distance. Take a step back and consider how that person must be feeling before you judge them. Also, remember that none of us are without sin. Ask God to help you to see others through his eyes.

———————————————————————————————

———————————————————————————————

———————————————————————————————

———————————————————————————————

———————————————————————————————

———————————————————————————————

———————————————————————————————

I will learn one scripture every week.

2 TIMOTHY 2:15 (NKJV)
Be diligent to present yourself approved
unto God, a worker who does not need to be
ashamed, rightly dividing the word of truth.

God longs for us to get closer to him. He designed
us to be in communion with him and to learn his
precepts. Reading his word daily and praying are the
best ways to do this. Create a fun and interactive way
for you to comprehend and memorize a new scripture
each week. It is important that you not only memorize
it but that you truly understand its meaning.

_____

_____

_____

_____

_____

_____

_____

I will perfect my craft.

COLOSSIANS 3:23
And whatever you do, do it heartily, as to the Lord and not
to men, knowing that from the Lord you will receive the
reward of the inheritance; for you serve the Lord Christ.

When we develop and hone our skills, we give God
glory. How? Because he gave us the skills that we
possess. Therefore, by improving and perfecting
those skills, we take what he has given us to the next
level. What can you do today to improve a skill?

_____

_____

_____

_____

_____

_____

_____

_____

I will not accept mediocrity.

JOHN 10:10 (ESV)
The thief comes only to steal and kill and destroy. I came that they may have life and have it abundantly.

God wants the best for his children. He wants us to achieve great things for his name's sake. When we examine this, we realize that this leaves no room for mediocrity or subpar performance in any arena of our lives. God is a God of excellence and he wants us to walk in excellence. What has been mediocre in your life? What can you do to change this today?

_____

_____

_____

_____

_____

_____

_____

I will celebrate small victories.

GENESIS 1:1-4 (NIV)
In the beginning God created the heavens and the earth.
Now the earth was formless and empty, darkness was
over the surface of the deep, and the Spirit of God was
hovering over the waters. And God said, "Let there be
light," and there was light. God saw that the light was
good, and he separated the light from the darkness.

When we achieve something, no matter how big or
how small, we are acknowledging our progress. In
acknowledging small progress, we encourage ourselves
to continue and achieve even greater progress. Even
God celebrated small victories when he saw that
"it was good" when he created each aspect of the
Earth. What small victories have you achieved in the
last week? Find a way to celebrate them today!

_____

_____

_____

_____

_____

I will not be afraid of money.

ECCLESIASTES 7:12 (KJV)
For wisdom *is* a defence, *and* money *is* a
defence: but the excellency of knowledge *is, that*
wisdom giveth life to them that have it.

God does not want us to be afraid of anything,
especially money. Money is supposed to bless us and
help us to bless others. Examine your relationship
with money today. Are you afraid of it? If so, why?

_____

_____

_____

_____

_____

_____

_____

_____

I will express gratitude each morning.

PSALM 118:24 (NLT)
This is the day the Lord has made. We
will rejoice and be glad in it.

Gratitude is such a powerful concept. When we express
our gratitude to God, we deepen our connection with
him by showing him that we appreciate his blessings
in our lives. It also sets a positive mood and tone
in your mind and spirit. For the next seven days, I
challenge you to practice expressing gratitude every
morning before you start your day. Pay close attention
to how starting your day with the expression of
gratitude affects your attitude throughout the day.

I will not complain and I will pray for those who do.

JAMES 5:9 (NASB)
Do not complain, brethren, against one another,
so that you yourselves may not be judged; behold,
the Judge is standing right at the door.

Complaining is a counterproductive use of energy.
If you find yourself complaining about something
today, I challenge you to turn that thought or
those words into something positive. For example,
if you feel like saying "I hate my job," instead
say, "God, I thank you for employment."

_____

_____

_____

_____

_____

_____

_____

I will show grace to others.

LUKE 6:35 (NKJV)
But love your enemies, do good, and lend, hoping
for nothing in return; and your reward will be
great, and you will be sons of the Most High.
For He is kind to the unthankful and evil.

We've named it the Golden Rule. It is one of the most
widely quoted scriptures and sayings. It is so simple and
yet so poignant. If we govern ourselves with this simple
principle, we will indeed begin practicing more kindness
and love in our daily interactions with others. Do you
treat others the way you want to be treated every day?

_____

_____

_____

_____

_____

_____

_____

I will take action in creating new possibilities.

JAMES 2:17 (NIV)
In the same way, faith by itself, if it is not
accompanied by action, is dead.

How many times have you heard someone say, "I am
waiting on my blessing," or "I am waiting on God"? How
many times have you said these things? As believers,
we are supposed to wait on God; however, we should
not wait idly. God loves action and movement. He
has great plans to bless us and get behind our efforts.
We have to do our part by giving him effort to get
behind. What new possibility can you create today?

_____

_____

_____

_____

_____

_____

_____

February

FEBRUARY 1

I will seek help when I need it.

PSALM 22:19
But you, Lord, do not be far from me. You are
my strength; come quickly to help me.

How many times have you said or thought to yourself, "I
can handle this, I don't need help"? God is willing and able
to provide you with help through his word and through his
people. End your silent struggle today and don't hesitate
to reach out to a trusted source for what you need.

_____

_____

_____

_____

_____

_____

_____

_____

_____

I will learn how to accept a compliment.

ACTS 17:28

For in him we live and move and have our being. As some
of your own poets have said, "We are His offspring."

When someone pays you a compliment, whether they are
aware or not, they are recognizing an attribute of God in
you. Everything that is good in you is merely a reflection
of God's goodness. So accept the compliment and thank
God for his goodness, which has manifested in you.

_____

_____

_____

_____

_____

_____

_____

_____

_____

_____

FEBRUARY 3

I will stop trying to be people's savior and
instead point them to the savior.

PSALM 66:16
Come and hear, all you who fear God; let
me tell you what he has done for me.

Have you ever had a friend or family member come to
you for advice on something that you weren't sure about?
This is the perfect situation for you to witness to them and
lead them to Christ. Who will you lead to Jesus today?

_____

_____

_____

_____

_____

_____

_____

_____

I am special, and the world needs my gift.

1 PETER 4:10
Each of you should use whatever gift you have
received to serve others, as faithful stewards
of God's grace in its various forms.

What gifts do you possess that no one knows about? When
God created you in your mother's womb, he gave you the
gifts that you possess. He did so for a reason and purpose.
How can you operate in your gifting, starting today?

_____

_____

_____

_____

_____

_____

_____

_____

_____

I am not in competition with anyone.

PHILIPPIANS 2:3-4 (ESV)
Do nothing from selfish ambition or conceit, but
in humility count others more significant than
yourselves. Let each of you look not only to his own
interests, but also to the interests of others.

Healthy competition can be good in certain
situations. Competition becomes unhealthy when
it becomes an obsession. Be sure that God is the
motivation for the things that you do. Use God as your
benchmark and you will remain on a good path.

_____

_____

_____

_____

_____

_____

_____

I will forgive what I have felt was unforgivable.

MATTHEW 6:15 (NIV)
But if you do not forgive others their sins,
your Father will not forgive your sins.

Has someone ever hurt you so deeply that you thought
to yourself, "I will never forgive them"? I challenge you
to forgive someone who has hurt you right now. Say out
loud, "I forgive X for X." You can fill in the blanks here,
but the main thing is that you release those feelings of
anger. Holding a grudge against someone does absolutely
nothing to them, but it can do a lot of damage to you.

I will not boast in my own abilities.

EPHESIANS 2:8-9
For it is by grace you have been saved, through faith—and this is not from yourselves, it is the gift of God—not by works, so that no one can boast.

God is the source of every good in our lives. Every blessing, no matter how big or small, comes directly from God. Of course he commands us to walk in confidence, however, it is important to always remember that he is the source. If you are going to boast or brag, boast or brag about him!

_____

_____

_____

_____

_____

_____

_____

_____

I will pray for my enemies.

LUKE 6:27-28
But to you who are listening I say: Love your enemies,
do good to those who hate you, bless those who
curse you, pray for those who mistreat you.

This commandment is perhaps one of the most difficult
that God gives us. Why do we have to pray for people
who hate us? Why do we have to be kind to people when
they mistreat us? The simple answer is because we
are disciples of Christ, therefore, we have to conduct
ourselves as he would. When we pray for those who
have wronged us, we invite God to work on us and on
them. What enemy will you uplift in prayer today?

_____

_____

_____

_____

_____

_____

I will not give in to temptation.

LUKE 22:40
On reaching the place, he said to them, "Pray
that you will not fall into temptation."

Temptation can come in many forms. When we
don't give in to temptation, we strengthen our spirit
by feeding it rather than feeding our flesh. When
you resist temptation, thank God for victory, and
celebrate! What temptation will you resist today?

_____

_____

_____

_____

_____

_____

_____

I will stop pretending to be perfect and be authentically me.

1 SAMUEL 16:7 (ESV)
But the Lord said to Samuel, "Do not look on
his appearance or on the height of his stature,
because I have rejected him. For the Lord sees
not as man sees: man looks on the outward
appearance, but the Lord looks on the heart."

Accept the fact that to be human is to be imperfect. When
you realize this, you will no longer feel the need to pretend.
God is concerned about the condition of your heart and
he does not expect perfection from us. Free yourself from
the notion that you cannot make mistakes, starting today!

I will stop magnifying my problems
and minimizing my God.
–Alexandria L. Barlowe

JEREMIAH 32:27
Behold, I am the Lord, the God of all
flesh. Is anything too hard for me?

How much time do we spend agonizing over our problems
as opposed to taking them to God in prayer? Choosing
to pray instead of worry is much easier said than done.
However, this is how God has called us to handle the
various issues that arise in our lives. Magnify God in
your life and watch him handle each and every problem
you face. Will you choose to magnify God today?

_____

_____

_____

_____

_____

_____

I will spend fifteen minutes in prayer and meditation today.

JAMES 4:8
Come near to God and he will come near
to you. Wash your hands, you sinners, and
purify your hearts, you double-minded.

In any relationship, the more time you spend nurturing
it, the better it will become. This is also true with our
relationship with God. During your fifteen-minute
prayer and meditation time today, ask him to give you
a desire for his word. Watch God work wonders when
you dedicate time for him in your daily schedule.

_____

_____

_____

_____

_____

_____

_____

I will write down my goals and give them a completion date.

HABAKKUK 2:2 (NKJV)
Then the Lord answered me and said: "Write the vision
and make it plain on tablets, that he may run who reads it.

A goal without a plan is a wish. How many times have you
set a goal and not followed through with it? I challenge
you to write down a goal and list two to three time-
specific steps that you will take to reach that goal. Once
you have accomplished one goal, you will find that you
are motivated to complete another. Keep up this pattern,
and before you know it, you will have accomplished all
of your goals. Then, it will be time to set new ones!

_____

_____

_____

_____

_____

_____

_____

I love me.

1 CORINTHIANS 13:13 (NIV)
And now these three remain: faith, hope and
love. But the greatest of these is love.

Depending on which version you read, love is mentioned
over five hundred times in the Bible. Take time to
think about what love means to you. Examine the
people and things you love. I challenge you to make a
list of all the things you love about yourself today.

_____

_____

_____

_____

_____

_____

_____

_____

_____

I will exercise and make healthy food choices today.

1 CORINTHIANS 3:16-17

Don't you know that you yourselves are God's temple and that God's Spirit dwells in your midst? If anyone destroys God's temple, God will destroy that person; for God's temple is sacred, and you together are that temple.

Making a lifestyle change is like learning to walk. You have to learn how to put one foot in front of the other. Babies have to master the art of walking long before they can run. The same can be said for trying to create healthy habits. Start today. Then do the same thing tomorrow and the day after that. We are in control of our activity level and what we put in our bodies. Honor God with your choices today.

_____

_____

_____

_____

_____

_____

I will not take part in gossip.

PROVERBS 15:1 (ESV)
A soft answer turns away wrath, but
a harsh word stirs up anger.

In a day and time when gossip is some people's livelihood, this can be a challenging thing to stick to. However, we must remember that not only is gossip a distraction, but it also can be very hurtful and even damaging to someone's reputation. If someone comes to you with gossip today, do not engage them. Either tell them that you have to go or find a way to change the subject.

I will not give up on my dream.

JOB 6:8 (NIV)
Oh, that I might have my request, that
God would grant what I hope for.

Have you been struggling with unbelief regarding your
dreams? Have you been asking God for a sign that you
are on the right path? Well, this is that sign! God wants
us to go after our dreams with tenacity. He gave us
the desires that we have, not for us to just think about
them but to put action behind those thoughts and make
them come to pass. Regardless of how many times
you've failed or how difficult you think it will be, never
give up on something that you are passionate about.

_____

_____

_____

_____

_____

_____

God wants to bless me.

3 JOHN 1:2
Dear friend, I pray that you may enjoy good
health and that all may go well with you,
even as your soul is getting along well.

God is not a bully in the sky! He is a loving father who
wants the best for his children. That includes you!
It blesses him to see us blessed. If you find yourself
feeling stress or anxiety about a particular situation or
thing today, remember that God wants to bless you.

I will not compromise who I am.

TITUS 2:11-12

For the grace of God has appeared that offers salvation
to all people. It teaches us to say "No" to ungodliness
and worldly passions, and to live self-controlled,
upright and godly lives in this present age.

God has called us to walk in integrity. It can be difficult to
be true to who you are, especially when your beliefs are
challenged or ridiculed. God did not compromise who
he was when he was faced with the greatest temptation.
Will you compromise your beliefs if given the chance?

I will be part of the solution, not the problem.

MATTHEW 7:7 (NASB)
Ask, and it will be given to you; seek, and you will
find; knock, and it will be opened to you.

Have you ever been around someone who constantly
complained about a certain situation? Complaining or
worrying is like sitting in a rocking chair: it gives you
something to do but gets you nowhere. I challenge
you to find ways to be solution oriented today.

I will look for opportunities to serve.

1 CORINTHIANS 12:5 (NIV)
There are different kinds of service, but the same Lord.

Whether it be your time, your money, your expertise, or other resources that are available to you, there are always ways to be of service. When we serve others, we are extending God's love to them. Who and how will you serve today?

I will activate my faith and LEAP!

JAMES 2:26
As the body without the spirit is dead,
so faith without deeds is dead.

As Christians, we know how crucial faith is to our walks with God. Did you know that works, actions, and deeds are all just as important? They are! As the body of Christ, we have to realize that having faith is only half the battle. We cannot use faith as an excuse for inaction. Your blessings are not going to fall from the sky and land gracefully in your lap! They will come from your efforts, so get to work! How will you activate your faith today?

I will spread love, not hate.

JOHN 15:17
This is my command: Love each other.

When we are angry, spreading love is much easier said than done. When you find yourself typing an angry email to that colleague who messed up on a project—for the umpteenth time—stop yourself. Are you operating out of love, as Christ commanded us to? Delete that email and start over. Ask God to help you find the words to correct your colleague in love, not in hate or anger. How many ways can you spread love today?

_____

_____

_____

_____

_____

_____

_____

I will be a better parent.

PROVERBS 22:6 (NASB)
Train up a child in the way he should go: and
when he is old, he will not depart from it.

Have you spent quality time with your children
today? There is no work project or deadline that is
more crucial than the emotional well-being of your
child. We live in a society that glorifies being mind-
numbingly busy. While it is good to have things that
require our attention in a work setting, your children
also require your attention. Ask God to guide you and
help you to be the parent that your children need.
Start small by finding a way to spend thirty minutes of
uninterrupted time with your children this evening.

_____

_____

_____

_____

_____

_____

I will be a loyal friend.

PROVERBS 18:24 (NIV)
One who has unreliable friends soon comes to ruin,
but there is a friend who sticks closer than a brother.

Our world places a heavy emphasis on independence.
While independence is vital to survival, friendships
with like-minded people are also vital. God made us to
relate and connect to others. If you are fortunate enough
to have even just one true friend, value them. Respect
and cherish them. Encourage and uplift them. Pray for
them. Defend them when applicable and necessary.

_____

_____

_____

_____

_____

_____

_____

FEBRUARY 26

I will always trust the promises of God.

2 CORINTHIANS 1:19-20 (NKJV)

For the Son of God, Jesus Christ, who was preached among you by us—by me, Silvanus, and Timothy—was not yes and no, but in Him was Yes. For all the promises of God in Him are Yes and in Him Amen, to the glory of God through us.

You read them with some regularity. You hear about them one to two times per week at church. You may even discuss them with friends and family members. But do you really truly trust God's promises? Do you believe that they will come to pass in your life, or are you just going through the motions when you read his word? His promises take on a whole new meaning when you make them personal and actually believe that they are for you! I challenge you to insert yourself in the next scripture you read. For example, blessed shall be the fruit of my body. Watch things happen for you when you start to believe!

_____

_____

_____

_____

_____

I will step out of my comfort zone.

JOSHUA 1:9 (ESV)
Have I not commanded you? Be strong and courageous.
Do not be frightened, and do not be dismayed, for
the Lord your God is with you wherever you go.

What is holding you back from greatness? If you answer
this question, you'll more than likely find that fear is
the root of what is holding you back. Don't be afraid of
doing something you have never done! No one likes to
feel uncomfortable, but you have to accept that what
you want is on the other side of your comfort zone! That
awesome business idea that you have been praying
about is on the other side of your comfort zone! How
uncomfortable are you willing to be to get to your
goals? What can you do to start on that path today?

I will pray for divine business connections.

2 CORINTHIANS 9:8 (NKJV)
And God is able to make all grace abound toward you,
that you, always having all sufficiency in all things,
may have an abundance for every good work.

Have you recently stepped out on faith to start a new
business venture but now find yourself wondering
where your sales are going to come from? You are not
alone. I challenge you to speak prosperity and good
success over your business. Tell God your concerns
about where your clients are going to come from.
God knows who you need to be connected to in order
to take your business to the next level. Find ways to
market your business and network. Be the best at
what you do and believe that God will do the rest!

_____

_____

_____

_____

_____

_____

March

I will expect God's favor.

PSALM 5:12 (NKJV)
For You, O Lord, will bless the righteous; with
favor You will surround him as with a shield.

When you expect something, you have full confidence
in it. You don't doubt or question it and you're not taken
aback when it happens. Why? Because you expected it.
We have to think of God's favor in this way. When we are
diligent, we must have full confidence that his favor will
find us and accomplish things on our behalf. We cannot
doubt or question that we will find favor in every arena
of our lives. Most importantly, do not be taken aback
when met with favor. You are a child of the King; favor
is to be expected. Just don't forget to thank him for it.

_____

_____

_____

_____

_____

_____

I am open to new ideas of wealth creation.

DEUTERONOMY 8:18 (ESV)
You shall remember the Lord your God, for it is he who gives you power to get wealth, that he may confirm his covenant that he swore to your fathers, as it is this day.

God wants his people to be blessed in their finances. Why? So that they can in turn bless others. It's an all-around win for you and God when you use your creativity to generate revenue streams. Think outside of the box! I challenge you to take fifteen minutes to brainstorm ideas that will increase you financially. They could be business ideas, management strategies, etc. Don't stop there. Take two to three of those ideas and create a realistic action plan to make them happen.

_____

_____

_____

_____

_____

_____

I will create my own paycheck.

MARK 5:36 (NIV)
Overhearing what they said, Jesus told
them, "Don't be afraid; just believe."

Do you believe that you can create your own paycheck?
What obstacles are in your way? When we are in control
of our own financial destiny, often, we are in control
of our time. Are you growing weary of your nine-to-
five job? Repeat this scripture to yourself every time
you find yourself feeling afraid to take control of your
financial well-being. Don't be afraid, just believe.

_____

_____

_____

_____

_____

_____

_____

I will look at money as a resource, not the source.

1 TIMOTHY 6:10

For the love of money is a root of all kinds of evil.
Some people, eager for money, have wandered from
the faith and pierced themselves with many griefs.

This is one of the most widely misunderstood scriptures
of the Bible. Many people confuse money with the love
of money. Money is not the root of all evil; the improper
love for it is. Money is obviously necessary for us to
live, but realize that Christ Jesus is our true source.
He is the source of everything. Have you placed money
in the right place in your life? If not, repent and ask
God to give you a healthy perspective on money.

_____

_____

_____

_____

_____

_____

I am ready to accept what God has for me.

PROVERBS 19:21 (ESV)
Many are the plans in the mind of a man, but it
is the purpose of the Lord that will stand.

God has a plan for your life. As you dive in and learn
more about his word, you will learn more about
what that plan looks like. Ask God to help you to
accept not only his blessings but also his plans.

I will be around people who inspire me.

PROVERBS 27:17 (NIV)
As iron sharpens iron, so one person sharpens another.

Does your current circle of friends inspire you? Do
they challenge you to be the best you that you can be?
If so, you are fortunate. Having the right people in your
inner circle can make or break you. Make an effort to
spend time with someone who inspires you today.

_____

_____

_____

_____

_____

_____

_____

_____

_____

I will not allow debt to rob me of my freedom.

DEUTERONOMY 15:6 (NASB)
For the Lord your God will bless you as He has
promised you, and you will lend to many nations,
but you will not borrow; and you will rule over
many nations, but they will not rule over you.

Debt is one of the most oppressive forces that plague our
nation. God wants you to live a life of freedom. Ask him
to give you the discipline and resources to live debt free.
Overcoming debt can be a long journey, but it is possible.
What step can you take toward living a debt-free life today?

_____

_____

_____

_____

_____

_____

_____

I will overcome my childhood hurts.

JAMES 1:2 (NIV)
Consider it pure joy, my brothers and sisters,
whenever you face trials of many kinds.

How can you consider your painful experiences to
be joy? You may be wondering how that is possible
after reading this scripture. The more you learn about
God's character, the more you will understand that
the things that have hurt you the most were designed
to strengthen you. Take comfort in knowing that your
childhood hang-ups don't define you. Ask God to heal
your heart of the things that hurt you in your childhood.

_____

_____

_____

_____

_____

_____

_____

_____

MARCH 9

I will laugh more.

PROVERBS 17:22 (KJV2000)
A merry heart does good like a medicine:
but a broken spirit dries the bones.

When is the last time you experienced hysterical
laughter? Lighten up the mood with a laugh today. Is
there a blog or television show that makes you laugh?
Take some time to watch it. There is truly no better
remedy for sadness or stress than a good laugh.

_____

_____

_____

_____

_____

_____

_____

_____

_____

I will leave a legacy of giving.

LUKE 6:38 (NASB)
Give, and it will be given to you. They will pour into your lap a good measure—pressed down, shaken together, and running over. For by your standard of measure it will be measured to you in return.

Generosity shares God's love with both the giver and the receiver. Be so impactful in your giving that your name becomes synonymous with it. Tell God what you need in order to give more. What can you give today?

_____

_____

_____

_____

_____

_____

_____

_____

I will not be defensive when someone
gives me constructive criticism.

PROVERBS 12:1 (ESV)
Whoever loves discipline loves knowledge,
but he who hates reproof is stupid.

Constructive criticism is one of the best ways that we can
learn and better ourselves. Being defensive prevents you
from receiving the help you need to improve. I challenge
you to thank the next person who offers pointers or
suggestions. Take what they say and use it to improve.

_____

_____

_____

_____

_____

_____

_____

_____

I do not need man's permission to do
what God has purposed me to do.

MATTHEW 5:14-15 (NKJV)
You are the light of the world. A city that is set on
a hill cannot be hidden. Nor do they light a lamp
and put it under a basket, but on a lampstand,
and it gives light to all who are in the house.

God wants you to live out your purpose without concern
of what others may think or say. When God has called you
to do something, don't wait for the approval or permission
of people. You have all the permission you need in God!

_____

_____

_____

_____

_____

_____

_____

I will not play "keeping up with the Joneses."

GALATIANS 6:4-5 (GWT)
Each of you must examine your own actions. Then you can be proud of your own accomplishments without comparing yourself to others. Assume your own responsibility.

Do you constantly compare yourself to friends on social media? Or maybe a sibling who always seems to have the upper hand on everything? Theodore Roosevelt once said that comparison is the thief of joy. Know that what God has for you is for you. It is in no way dependent on what your neighbor has. The next time you catch yourself comparing yourself to someone else, stop and tell yourself "what God has for me is for me."

_____

_____

_____

_____

_____

_____

MARCH 14

I will practice positive self-talk.

PROVERBS 18:21 (ESV)
Death and life are in the power of the tongue,
and those who love it will eat its fruit.

When you speak words of positivity to yourself, it changes
your pattern of thinking. Tell yourself that you can do
it instead of saying that you cannot. Even if you do not
believe you can, the power of positive speaking can
propel you forward. Speak that you are able to achieve,
and eventually, you will start to believe what you are
saying. On the converse, if you constantly tell yourself
that you can't do it, you will continue to believe that.

_____

_____

_____

_____

_____

_____

_____

MARCH 15

I will invest quality time in self-care.

PSALM 127:2 (NKJV)
It is vain for you to rise up early, to sit up late, and to eat the bread of sorrows; for so He gives His beloved sleep.

God knows that our minds and bodies need rest. Often, we don't take enough time for ourselves to unplug so that we can return refreshed and recharged. Break that habit starting today. What will you do to care for yourself today?

_____

_____

_____

_____

_____

_____

_____

_____

I choose to be happy no matter what.

PSALM 92:4 (NASB)
For you, O Lord, have made me glad by what You have done, I will sing for joy at the works of Your hands.

It takes a great deal of mental toughness to choose to be happy when all hell is breaking loose in your life. We must remember that happiness truly is a choice. Even when it is a difficult choice to make, choose happiness. Always choose happiness!

_____

_____

_____

_____

_____

_____

_____

_____

MARCH 17

I matter to me.

Luke 12:6-7 (ESV)
Are not five sparrows sold for two pennies? And
not one of them is forgotten before God. Why, even
the hairs on your head are all numbered. Fear not;
you are of more value than many sparrows.

You matter to God more than you could ever know.
You need to matter to you, too. Show yourself that
you matter by speaking up for yourself, being true
to your feelings, and not allowing yourself to be
mistreated. You are God's creation. You owe it to him
to value what he has made and called his own.

I will walk in greatness.

JOB 37:5 (ESV)
God thunders wondrously with his voice; he does
great things that we cannot comprehend.

Merriam Webster defines greatness in this context as
"markedly superior in character or quality; especially noble
or remarkably skilled." Take a minute or two to read that
definition again and let it sink in. Your heavenly father is
nothing less than great. He created you in his likeness. So
what does that say about you? Keep this definition in mind
throughout the day, especially if something causes you to
lose confidence in yourself or your abilities. Remember that
you are a child of the King and nothing less than great!

_____

_____

_____

_____

_____

_____

Somebody needs my gift.

ROMANS 12:6 (ESV)
Having gifts that differ according to the grace given to us, let us use them: if prophecy in proportion to our faith.

Would you believe me if I told you that there is someone in the world right now who is in search of the gifts you possess? It's the truth. Ask God to direct your path to someone who could benefit from your gift. In using that gift, you will bring glory to God. I challenge you to seek out an opportunity to be a blessing to someone using your gift today.

I will change the atmosphere in the room.

PSALM 16:11 (NASB)
You will make known to me the path of life;
In Your presence is fullness of joy; In Your
right hand there are pleasures forever.

Just as there is fullness of joy in God's presence,
there should be a definite difference in our presence
as well. You should not have to announce that you
are a Believer—people should already know by
your presence and how you conduct yourself. Pray
that God's character shines through you and that it
touches everyone you come in contact with today.

_____

_____

_____

_____

_____

_____

_____

I will be in radical action.

JAMES 1:23-25 (ESV)

For if anyone is a hearer of the word and not a doer, he is like a man who looks intently at his natural face in a mirror. For he looks at himself and goes away and at once forgets what he was like. But the one who looks into the perfect law, the law of liberty and perseveres, being no hearer who forgets but a doer who acts, he will be blessed in his doing.

God is a God of action! His word commands us to put action to work with our faith. Is there something that has been on your heart or mind that you have failed to act on? I challenge you to take action on that matter today!

_____

_____

_____

_____

_____

_____

_____

Hearing "no" will not stop me from reaching my goals.

COLOSSIANS 1:11-12 (NIV)
Being strengthened with all power according to his
glorious might so that you may have great endurance
and patience, and giving joyful thanks to the Father,
who has qualified you to share in the inheritance
of his holy people in the kingdom of light.

Rejection is never pleasant, especially when it involves
something that we worked very hard for. You must take
comfort in the fact that a delay is not a denial. Every "no"
is getting you one step closer to a "yes"! Be persistent in
your pursuits and watch God get behind your efforts!

I will not be distracted by anything or anyone.

PHILIPPIANS 3:13-14 (NKJV)
Brethren, I do not count myself to have apprehended;
but one thing I do, forgetting those things which
are behind and reaching forward to those things
which are ahead, I press toward the goal for the
prize of the upward call of God in Christ Jesus.

The enemy loves nothing more than distracting us
with whatever and whoever he can. He pulls out
all of the stops when it comes to getting children
of God off track and focused on things that don't
bring God glory. Before you react to something that
upsets you today, ask yourself if it is a distraction.

_____

_____

_____

_____

_____

_____

I will be selective about the advice I receive.

PROVERBS 15:31-33 (NKJV)
The ear that hears the rebukes of life will abide among the wise. He who disdains instruction despises his own soul, but he who heeds rebuke gets understanding. The fear of the Lord is the instruction of wisdom, and before honor is humility.

God tells us that good advice can lengthen our days. Just as good advice adds to our life, bad advice subtracts from it. When seeking advice, be sure that the person you go to has already achieved what you are inquiring about. Also, be sure that person can give you Godly counsel. Make a list of people who you can go to for good advice and a list of people who you don't feel would give you good advice. Keep the lists handy for when you need to remind yourself of who you can turn to.

I will stop telling myself what I cannot do.

Romans 4:17 (NKJV)
(As it is written, "I have made you a father of many
nations") in the presence of Him whom he believed–
God, who gives life to the dead and calls those
things which do not exist as though they did.

If you tell yourself that you can't, you won't. Tell yourself
that you can and you will! Activate positivity and believe
that you can and will accomplish whatever it is that you set
out to do. What will you tell yourself that you can do today?

_____

_____

_____

_____

_____

_____

_____

_____

I will freely compliment others.

PROVERBS 12:25 (KJV2000)
Heaviness in the heart of man makes him
stoop: but a good word makes him glad.

Paying someone a genuine compliment is like
spreading a little love every time you do it. Wouldn't
you love to know that your kind words to someone
were right on time and exactly what they needed
to hear? You can be that person. I challenge you to
compliment as many people as you can today.

I will accept assistance from others.

JAMES 1:17 (NIV)
Every good and perfect gift is from above, coming down from the Father of the heavenly lights, who does not change like shifting shadows.

Help when we need it is truly a gift from God. Do not let your pride interfere with that gift. Whether it be financial assistance or just a listening ear during a challenging time, know that those who want to help are doing God's work. Let them do so.

I will not share what others have told me in confidence.

PROVERBS 11:13 (ESV)
Whoever goes about slandering reveals secrets, but he
who is trustworthy in spirit keeps a thing covered.

Have you ever found out that something you told a friend
in confidence was told to someone else? How did that
make you feel? Did you continue to trust that person
with personal information? When confidence is broken,
trust is violated. Without trust, a healthy relationship
cannot exist. Remember to value your friendships
enough to be a keeper of secrets if a friend or family
member has told you something in confidence.

_____

_____

_____

_____

_____

_____

_____

I will be loyal to my friends.

PROVERBS 20:6 (NKJV)
Most men will proclaim each his own goodness,
but who can find a faithful man?

A loyal friend is a gift from God. We bless our friends
when we are loyal to them, and in turn, we are blessed
by their loyalty to us. Take a few minutes to pray for the
people who have proved themselves to be loyal to you. Also,
pray that God helps you to continue to be a loyal friend.

_____

_____

_____

_____

_____

_____

_____

_____

_____

I will call the person who keeps coming to mind.

PROVERBS 17:17 (NIV)
A friend loves at all times, and a brother
is born for a time of adversity.

Do you have a friend whom you haven't spoken
to in a while? Do you keep telling yourself that
you are going to call them and see how they are
doing? Call them today. Checking on a friend can
go a long way and show them that you care.

_____

_____

_____

_____

_____

_____

_____

_____

_____

I will not fulfill the lusts of my flesh.

ROMANS 13:14 (ESV)
But put on the Lord Jesus Christ, and make no
provision for the flesh, to gratify its desires.

Lust is one of the most effective tools of the enemy.
Our flesh is weak, and we need the strength of God
to keep from giving in to lust. When we feed our
spirit, it becomes stronger than our flesh and allows
us to be better equipped against lust. Learn your lust
triggers and remove yourself from them. Don't place
yourself in a position to succumb to your flesh.

April

I will begin to pay off my debt today.

ROMANS 13:8 (NASB)
Owe nothing to anyone except to love one another;
for he who loves his neighbor has fulfilled the law.

If you are in debt, the most important thing you can
do is create an action plan to get out of it. Depending
on the amount of debt you are in, it can be a long
process, but the financial freedom is absolutely
worth it. Call a creditor today and set up a payment
plan. No matter how small the amount is, stick to
those monthly payments. You can be debt free!

I will pray for others consistently.

EPHESIANS 6:18 (NASB)
With all prayer and petition pray at all times in the
Spirit, and with this in view, be on the alert with
all perseverance and petition for all the saints.

Everyone you know is fighting some sort of personal
battle. Whether it be big or small, they need your
prayers. Learn to pray for others just as you want
them to pray for you. Make a list of your friends and
family members and uplift them in prayer today.

_____

_____

_____

_____

_____

_____

_____

I will not participate in sowing discord.

ROMANS 16:17 (ESV)
I appeal to you, brothers, to watch out for those who cause divisions and create obstacles contrary to the doctrine that you have been taught; avoid them.

When we participate in any activity that disrupts harmony, we are not bringing God glory. We are doing the exact opposite. Sometimes we participate unknowingly. Always be careful to remove yourself from this type of situation. How will you avoid discord sowing today? How will you respond to someone in your midst who is sowing discord?

I will guard my heart from greed.

PROVERBS 1:19 (KJV2000)
So are the ways of every one that is greedy of
gain; which takes away the life of its owners.

One of the seven deadly sins, greed, seems to be a
common staple in popular culture. God has not called us
to be insatiable in our desire for material or monetary
gain. Greed causes one to never be satisfied and always
wanting more, regardless of what they already have. Cast
greed out of your life today. Ask to fill the voids in your life
instead of attempting to fill them with materialistic gain.

_____

_____

_____

_____

_____

_____

_____

I will not allow a diagnosis to dictate my destiny.
–Alexandria L. Barlowe

PSALM 112:7 (NIV)
They will have no fear of bad news; their
hearts are steadfast, trusting in the Lord.

Getting a bad report from the doctor is not something that
any of us want to experience. There is even a nickname
for anxiety that is onset by going to the doctor: white coat
syndrome. Fear not. You are a child of the Chief Physician.
Even if you have received a devastating report from your
doctor, the fact that you are breathing in this moment
should let you know that there is still hope and time for
God to have the final say. I believe in agreement with you
for the full and complete restoration of your health.

_____

_____

_____

_____

_____

_____

I will spend more time doing things that make me happy.

2 CHRONICLES 9:7 (NIV)
How happy your people must be! How happy your officials,
who continually stand before you and hear your wisdom!

Our happiness glorifies God! When his children are
happy, he is happy! What is one thing that makes
you happy? When is the last time you did that? Find
thirty minutes in your day today to do just that.

_____

_____

_____

_____

_____

_____

_____

_____

I will take full responsibility for my actions.

GALATIANS 6:5 (KJV2000)
For every man shall bear his own burden.

When God created us, he gave us free will, or the
ability to make our own decisions. Know that you are
in total control over what you say and do. Also, know
that our actions come with consequences. It is common
for us to say things like "you made me do this," but
the truth is, no one can truly make us do anything.
We have a God-given ability to choose our actions.

I am a maintainer of peace.

MATTHEW 5:9 (ESV)
Blessed are the peacemakers, for they
shall be called sons of God.

Would you like to do God's work today? You can by
keeping the peace in a situation that has become
anything but peaceful. God loves when we do our
part to end conflict or help two quarreling people
come to an agreement. What will you do the next
time you are placed in the position of peacemaker?

I will accept the fact that true joy can
only be found in Jesus Christ.

1 PETER 1:8-9 (NIV)
Though you have not seen him, you love him; and
even though you do not see him now, you believe
in him and are filled with an inexpressible and
glorious joy, for you are receiving the end result
of your faith, the salvation of your souls.

Have you ever tried to plug a three-pronged chord
into a two-prong outlet? Were you frustrated by the
fact that the cord would not fit? The same can be said
when we search for joy in anything or anyone other
than God. People will always let us down. That is part
of what it means to be human, but God will never
leave or forsake us. I challenge you to end your search
today and allow God to fill the voids in your life.

_____

_____

_____

_____

_____

APRIL 10

I am successful in what I do.

JOSHUA 1:8 (NKJV)
This Book of the Law shall not depart from your
mouth, but you shall meditate in it day and night,
that you may observe to do according to all that
is written in it. For then you will make your way
prosperous, and then you will have good success.

God's word is our key to success. In his word,
we can find all of the answers and tools that we
need to succeed. Will you use your key today?

_____

_____

_____

_____

_____

_____

_____

APRIL 11

I will not live above my means.

ECCLESIASTES 5:10 (NIV)
Whoever loves money never has enough;
whoever loves wealth is never satisfied with
their income. This too is meaningless.

Overspending is usually the result of lack. Lack of
resources, lack of planning, lack of discipline, etc. There
can be many reasons why we overspend, but God has
called us to be wise with our finances. Seek out wisdom
on how you can live within or beneath your means
and establish a workable plan for your finances.

I will make beautiful memories
instead of purchasing things.

PROVERBS 10:7 (NASB)
The memory of the righteous is blessed,
but the name of the wicked will rot.

Material things can be destroyed, but memories cannot.
Do not replace the opportunity to spend precious
time with a loved one with buying them instead. Gifts
are great, but time is even better. What beautiful
memory will you make with a loved one today?

I will put my trust in God.

PSALM 9:10

Those who know your name trust in you, for you,
Lord, have never forsaken those who seek you.

God yearns for our trust in him. He designs situations
in our lives to teach us how to trust him. Placing trust
in him gives us a sense of peace. Surrender every
burden to God in prayer. Allow him to do your heavy
lifting. He wants to be your solution. Will you let him?

I will remain faithful in my marriage.

PROVERBS 5:15 (GNT)
Be faithful to your own wife and give your love to her alone.

God designed the institution of marriage to symbolize our relationship with him and also to provide us with companionship in covenant. Adultery severs that covenant and breaks the vows that are recited when a couple marries. Life tests every marriage, but being faithful to your spouse is about honoring God as well as keeping your vow. Guard your heart and your home from all forces that seek to tempt either spouse to be unfaithful.

_____

_____

_____

_____

_____

_____

_____

APRIL 15

I will do my very best.

ECCLESIASTES 9:10 (ESV)
Whatever your hand finds to do, do it with your
might, for there is no work or thought or knowledge
or wisdom in Sheol, to which you are going.

God wants us to give our best effort in everything we
do. As children of God, everything that we are part
of is an opportunity for God's light to shine through
us. We are his representatives and we should want
to represent him well. What can you do today to
show God that you are doing your very best?

_____

_____

_____

_____

_____

_____

_____

I will not carry my gifts to the grave.

1 TIMOTHY 4:14
Do not neglect the gift you have, which was
given you by prophecy when the council
of elders laid their hands on you.

Have you ever heard someone say "he or she has so much
potential"? Potential is an existing possibility that has
yet to be actualized. I don't know about you, but when
it is time for me to go on to the next life, I do not want
any remaining existing possibility to be unused. Are you
utilizing your gifts now or holding on to potential?

_____

_____

_____

_____

_____

_____

_____

APRIL 17

I will share my testimony with someone who needs it.

LUKE 8:39
"Return to your home, and declare how much God has done for you." And he went away, proclaiming throughout the whole city how much Jesus had done for him.

When we share our praise reports with others, faith in God's power becomes contagious. Hearing how God blessed you reminds others that he can and will do it for them too. Who will you share your testimony with today?

I will start my business today.

Psalm 20:4 (NIV)
May he give you the desire of your heart
and make all your plans succeed.

You've been thinking about it long enough. It's time
to activate! Make that phone call, schedule that
meeting, prepare that presentation. God desires to
help you succeed. Do your part by putting in the work
to get started. What action will you take today?

_____

_____

_____

_____

_____

_____

_____

_____

_____

I will save $25 this week.

PROVERBS 21:20
The wise store up choice food and olive
oil, but fools gulp theirs down.

How many times have you said, "I can't afford this?"
With good planning and saving, you can afford the things
you want or need. If you save $3.57 every day for seven
days, you will have saved $25 in one week. If you do this
every week for one year, you will have saved $1,300!
Saving money is not as difficult as you think. It could
mean skipping your morning coffee or favorite afternoon
snack, but it is so worth it. Will you save $3.57 today?

I will volunteer at a local organization.

TITUS 3:14
Our people must learn to devote themselves
to doing what is good, in order to provide for
urgent needs and not live unproductive lives.

Local food banks are always looking for volunteers
to help. Take friends and family along and make a
day's adventure of it. You may be surprised at how
much fun you have in doing so. We as the Body
of Christ are called to help those who are less
fortunate. What organization will you call today?

_____

_____

_____

_____

_____

_____

_____

APRIL 21

I will not walk in bitterness.

 EPHESIANS 4:31 (NKJV)
Let all bitterness, wrath, anger, clamor and evil
speaking be put away from you, along with all malice.

Has your heart hardened because someone you
trusted betrayed you? I challenge you to release those
feelings of bitterness and embrace God's grace and
forgiveness. Being bitter blocks your heart from
being able to receive and believe again. Don't stand
in your own way; bind the spirit of bitterness now!

_____

_____

_____

_____

_____

_____

_____

_____

I will focus on the things of God.

PHILIPPIANS 4:8
Finally, brothers and sisters, whatever is true, whatever
is noble, whatever is right, whatever is pure, whatever
is lovely, whatever is admirable—if anything is
excellent or praiseworthy—think about such things.

Whatever we think about is what we will end up
doing. Why? Because our thoughts serve as guides or
maps to the things that we value. If we are focused
on anything other than things of God, we are surely
headed for a path of actions that are not pleasing to
God. Have you been focusing on the things of God in
your life? If not, how will you shift your focus today?

_____

_____

_____

_____

_____

_____

I will not build myself up by tearing someone else down.

MATTHEW 15:11 (NKJV)
Not what goes into the mouth defiles a man; but
what comes out of the mouth, this defiles a man.

Have you ever been in a relationship where your partner
was constantly criticizing you while praising themselves?
Maybe this has happened to you in a work setting where
a colleague is always undermining your work while giving
himself credit for his? This type of emotional abuse is truly
damaging to one's psyche. God called us to be uplifters of
others, not the opposite. Be sure that you are encouraging
in your interactions with others. Never make the mistake
of thinking that putting someone else down builds you up.

I will complete tasks that I start.

PROVERBS 10:4 (NASB)
Poor is he who works with a negligent hand,
but the hand of the diligent makes rich.

Are you that person who starts ten projects but finishes
none of them? Trust me, you are not alone. However, if
we want to have order in our lives, we must finish what
we have started. What project will you complete today?

_____

_____

_____

_____

_____

_____

_____

_____

_____

I will be more patient.

JAMES 1:3 (KJV)
Knowing *this*, that the trying of your faith worketh patience.

How many times have we heard an elder family member tell us "patience is a virtue"? It's true! God embodied patience and he calls us to do so as well. The things that try your patience the most today are the things that will teach how to be more patient.

I will not be afraid of failing.

JEREMIAH 8:4
Moreover you shall say to them, "Thus says the Lord:
'Will they fall and not rise?
Will one turn away and not return?'"

At some point, we all fail at something. Although it can be discouraging, the most important thing is that you don't give up. Look at failure as an opportunity to learn and better yourself. So you opened your business and it failed. You can open it again. Don't give up, no matter how many times you've failed.

_____

_____

_____

_____

_____

_____

_____

I will believe that God's grace is for me.

2 CORINTHIANS 12:9 (NIV)
But he said to me, "My grace is sufficient for
you, for my power is made perfect in weakness."
Therefore I will boast all the more gladly about my
weaknesses, so that Christ's power may rest on me.

We don't have to give anything in return for it. We can't
buy it. We haven't earned it. It is a gift and it is a sufficient
gift. It is God's grace and the most precious gift that
we could receive. God has blessed all of his children
with his grace; it is simply up to you to believe it.

_____

_____

_____

_____

_____

_____

_____

APRIL 28

I will not be crippled by fear.

2 TIMOTHY 1:7 (NKJV)
For God has not given us a spirit of fear but of
power and of love and of a sound mind.

Fear can keep you frozen in a prison of inaction
if you allow it to. We all experience fear in things
that we are unfamiliar with. Know that God has
called you to be courageous. Anything that he has
brought you to, he will surely bring you through!

I will stop worrying about my future.

MATTHEW 6:34
Therefore, do not worry about tomorrow, for
tomorrow will worry about its own things.
Sufficient for the day is its own trouble.

Worry causes us to stress and to lose focus of God's
provision. Know that God always provides for his
children. Although things may seem bleak, rest
assured that he will supply your needs. Worrying
about tomorrow doesn't do anything for today.
Trust in God and sleep peacefully tonight.

_____

_____

_____

_____

_____

_____

_____

I will stop pretending to be publicly blessed
while I am privately in distress.

PSALM 118:5 (NASB)
From my distress I called upon the Lord; the Lord
answered me and set me in a large place.

God calls us to be honest and that includes being honest
with ourselves. Only our pride benefits from pretending to
be someone or something we are not. Pray that God fixes
what is broken in your life so that you no longer feel the
need to pretend or be anyone other than who you truly are.

May

I will cry if I need to.

JOEL 2:12
"Yet even now," declares the Lord, "Return to me with all
your heart, and with fasting, weeping and mourning."

Tears are an emotional release. Too often we are made
to feel as if crying is a sign of weakness, but this is not
true. God knows and understands our emotions and he
doesn't feel any different toward us because we cry when
we are sad, angry, or sometimes even happy. Whatever
the reason for your tears, don't hold back. Let them fall.

_____

_____

_____

_____

_____

_____

_____

_____

I will stop trying to change people and work on me.

1 THESSALONIANS 4:11 (NKJV)
That you also aspire to lead a quiet life, to
mind your own business, and to work with
your own hands, as we commanded you.

The only person we are able to change is the person who
stares back at us in the mirror. With God's help, others can
change, but they have to want it for themselves. How many
times have we heard someone say or said ourselves, "they
would be the perfect person if they just did this?" When
we redirect our efforts to being the change we hope to
see, we have better chances of achieving true happiness.

MAY 3

I will do something kind for someone unexpectedly.

EPHESIANS 4:32 (NASB)
Be kind to one another, tender-hearted, forgiving each
another, just as God in Christ also has forgiven you.

Have you ever seen someone's face light up after
receiving something unexpectedly? There are few
things that are more wonderful than someone's
reaction to a random gesture of thoughtfulness.
God calls us to act in kindness toward each other.
Who will you surprise with kindness today?

_____

_____

_____

_____

_____

_____

_____

_____

MAY 4

I will believe that God has good things in store for me.

1 CORINTHIANS 2:9 (NKJV)
But as it is written: "Eye has not seen, nor ear heard,
Nor have entered into the heart of man The things
which God has prepared for those who love Him."

Do you know how much God wants to bless
you? Most likely, as this scripture states, not
because we as man cannot even fathom all that
God has for us. Don't believe anything less.

_____

_____

_____

_____

_____

_____

_____

_____

_____

I will walk in the fact that I am his.

PSALM 24:1 (NKJV)
The earth is the Lord's, and its fullness, The
world, and those who dwell therein.

Do you know who you belong to? When we understand that
our Father created us and the world that we live in, we can
allow that to govern how we treat ourselves and how we
treat others. Are you walking in your heavenly lineage?

_____

_____

_____

_____

_____

_____

_____

_____

MAY 6

I will make sure my finances are in order.

LUKE 12:42 (NKJV)
And the Lord said, "Who then is that faithful and wise
steward, whom his master will make ruler over his
household, to give them their portion of food in due season?

God is a God of order. He does not reside where there
is chaos and disarray. By making sure our finances are
in order, we show God that we can be good stewards.
We also invite him to be a blessing to our finances.
What can you do to put your finances in order today?

_____

_____

_____

_____

_____

_____

_____

_____

I will give my children my undivided attention.

PSALM 127:3 (NIV)
Children are a heritage from the Lord,
offspring a reward from Him.

We most likely hear it all the time, but children truly are
a blessing! They are vibrant little human beings whom
God entrusted us to care for. They crave our attention
and thrive when we give it to them. Spend one hour
with your children without electronic devices today.

_____

_____

_____

_____

_____

_____

_____

_____

I am God's elect.

COLOSSIANS 3:12 (NKJV)
Therefore, as the elect of God, holy and
beloved, put on tender mercies, kindness,
humility, meekness, longsuffering.

To be chosen by God for salvation is not something to
be taken lightly or for granted. When he chose you, he
knew of your imperfections and shortcomings; and he still
chose you! You are enough to him, be enough for you!

_____

_____

_____

_____

_____

_____

_____

_____

I will give myself a second chance and if I
fail, I will give myself another one.

PROVERBS 24:16 (AKJV)
For a just man falls seven times, and rises up
again: but the wicked shall fall into mischief.

Isn't it a blessing to serve a God of second chances?
God wants you to succeed and he knows that
sometimes we have to lose in order to win. Don't
ever stop giving yourself another chance, no
matter how many "anothers" you require!

I will wait on the Lord.

PSALM 40:1 (NIV)
I waited patiently for the Lord; he
turned to me and heard my cry.

When we wait on God, we learn to trust in him
and increase our faith. Never doubt that God hears
your cries. Never doubt that he will come through
for you! Trust in him and wait on his promises.

_____

_____

_____

_____

_____

_____

_____

_____

I will inspire others.

1 THESSALONIANS 5:11 (ESV)
Therefore encourage one another and build
one another up, just as you are doing.

How can your words and actions be an inspiration
today? Think about things that inspire you.
Be the reason someone smiles today.

_____

_____

_____

_____

_____

_____

_____

_____

_____

I will share God's word with everyone
I come in contact with.

MARK 16:15 (BSB)
And He said to them, "Go into all the world
and preach the gospel to every creature."

One of our greatest duties as believers is to share God's word with others. You don't have to be a preacher or even be the most eloquent person to witness to someone. All you have to do is share your personal testimony with someone. Who will you bless with the gospel today?

_____

_____

_____

_____

_____

_____

_____

_____

I will be true to who God has called me to be.

ROMANS 1:6 (NASB)
Among whom you also are the called of Jesus Christ.

Who has God called you to be? In order to be true to who God has called you to be, you must first find out who God called you to be. Ask him to reveal this to you.

_____

_____

_____

_____

_____

_____

_____

_____

_____

_____

I will not make promises that I cannot keep.

NUMBERS 30:2 (ESV)
If a man makes a vow to the Lord, or swears an oath to bind himself by a pledge, he shall not break his word. He shall do according to all that proceeds out of his mouth.

One of the strongest things that we have is our word. God wants us to be men and women of our word. Be sure that you can deliver on something before promising it. If you cannot deliver, be honest about it. What promises will you reconsider making today?

_____

_____

_____

_____

_____

_____

_____

_____

I will add value to every project that I am a part of.

ECCLESIASTES 4:9 (ESV)
Two are better than one, because they
have a good reward for their toil.

You are brilliant. Your words and thoughts are relevant and much needed. When you are part of a project, that project is blessed because of your input. Walk in this today!

_____

_____

_____

_____

_____

_____

_____

_____

_____

_____

I will make a difference in this world.

HEBREWS 13:16 (NLT)
And don't forget to do good and to share with those
in need. These are the sacrifices that please God.

You are a difference maker! You can help cause change!
You are a generational curse breaker. You will leave
a great legacy in this world. Your essence matters to
God. He has called you to do great things! Are you
walking in God's plan and purpose for your life?

_____

_____

_____

_____

_____

_____

_____

_____

I will remain open to receive unexpected blessings.

EPHESIANS 3:20 (NIV)
Now to him who is able to do immeasurably
more than all we ask or imagine, according
to his power that is at work within us.

Don't ever doubt that God can surprise you with his
goodness! Don't be so accustomed to things not going
well that you stop believing or expecting. Remember that
God is all powerful and all knowing. In his time, he does
great things that can leave us in awe! Have you allowed
your situation to cause you to be in a place of unbelief?

MAY 18

I will not dim my light to make others feel
comfortable in their darkness.

MATTHEW 5:15 (NKJV)
Nor do they light a lamp and put it under a basket, but on
a lampstand, and it gives light to all who are in the house.

God's word says that he is the light of the world.
Don't allow darkness to cause you to feel as if
you need to change. Use your light to change
those who are in darkness. Never question God's
purpose for your life! How will you shine today?

I will stand on God's restoration power.

JOEL 2:25 (ESV)
I will restore to you the years that the swarming
locust has eaten, the hopper, the destroyer, and the
cutter, my great army, which I sent among you.

Is there a situation that is dead in your life? God specializes
in breathing life into things that seem to be dead—your
marriage, your finances, your business, etc. Whatever it
may be, God can and will restore it! Do you believe?

_____

_____

_____

_____

_____

_____

_____

_____

I will separate myself from confusion and pettiness.

1 CORINTHIANS 14:33
For God is not a God of confusion but of peace.
As in all the churches of the saints.

God calls us to flee from situations that do not
glorify him. Wherever there is confusion or
pettiness, God is not present. Do you have people
in your life who seem to always be surrounded by
confusion? Pray for them and be sure to avoid getting
involved in situations that breed confusion.

_____

_____

_____

_____

_____

_____

_____

_____

I will seek God's face before making decisions.

1 JOHN 5:14

And this is the confidence that we have toward him, that
if we ask anything according to his will he hears us.

Have you included God in your decision-making process?
God wants us to come to him with the issues that we face.
Don't forget to consult with him before making a choice.

I will credit people for their work.

HEBREWS 10:24-25
And let us consider how to stir up one
another to love and good works.

Praising someone when they have done something
well is a great way to show God's love. It will boost
their confidence and show that you acknowledge
them. Who can you give accolades to today?

_____

_____

_____

_____

_____

_____

_____

_____

_____

I will stand for what is right even if I am standing alone.

COLOSSIANS 1:23 (NASB)
If indeed you continue in the faith firmly established and steadfast, and not moved away from the hope of the gospel that you have heard, which was proclaimed in all creation under heaven, and of which I, Paul, was made a minister.

We are put in situations where we have to discern between right and wrong. These situations are never easy to deal with, but God allows us to be in these scenarios for a reason. Never be afraid to be the only person standing up for what is right.

I will not comment on things I know nothing about.

PROVERBS 29:20 (ESV)
Do you see a man who is hasty in his words?
There is more hope for a fool than for him.

God wants us to be wise in all that we do and especially
what we say. Be sure that you are knowledgeable
about a subject before speaking about it.

_____

_____

_____

_____

_____

_____

_____

_____

_____

_____

I will be a cheerful giver.

2 CORINTHIANS 9:7
Each one must give as he has decided in his
heart, not reluctantly or under compulsion,
for God loves a cheerful giver.

God loves when we give freely and happily. Ask
God to bless you with a giving heart so that you
will enjoy giving, if you do not already.

I will live like today is my last day.

MATTHEW 16:26
For what will it profit a man if he gains the
whole world and forfeits his soul? Or what
shall a man give in return for his soul?

What would you do if you were told that today was your
last day? That is a bit of a scary thought, but an even
scarier thought is leaving this earth with unfinished
business or unused potential! Ask God to help you use all
of your potential and to live each day as if it is your last.

_____

_____

_____

_____

_____

_____

_____

_____

I will speak positive words over my family.

EPHESIANS 4:29
Let no corrupting talk come out of your mouths,
but only such as is good for building up, as fits the
occasion, that it may give grace to those who hear.

It blesses your family when you speak positively
to them. It inspires them and lets them know how
much you love and care for them. What positive
words will you speak to your family today?

_____

_____

_____

_____

_____

_____

_____

I will stop holding on to dead things.

ISAIAH 43:18-19
Remember not the former things, nor consider the
things of old. Behold I am doing a new thing; now
it springs forth, do you not perceive it? I will make
a way in the wilderness and rivers in the desert.

Are you holding on to something that you need to let go of?
Dead weight makes our burdens that much heavier. Pray
that God gives you the strength to move on from those
things that are no longer serving you or giving him glory.

_____

_____

_____

_____

_____

_____

_____

_____

I will not be afraid to be vulnerable.

MATTHEW 5:5 (NIV)
Blessed are the meek, for they will inherit the earth.

This may seem counterintuitive, but there is great strength in being vulnerable. When we let our guard down with those we can trust, we allow for a deeper connection with them. What situation will you be vulnerable in today?

_____

_____

_____

_____

_____

_____

_____

_____

_____

I will remove toxic people from my life.

PSALM 1:1
Blessed is the one who does not walk in step
with the wicked or stand in the way that sinners
take or sit in the company of mockers.

Is there someone in your life who encourages you to
do wrong? Laughs at you when you fail as opposed
to encouraging you? I pray that God cleanses your
life of all bad influences! Bad company brings bad
things. Don't be afraid to do some "spring cleaning"
where necessary among your friends list.

I will stop feeling sorry for myself.

1 THESSALONIANS 5:18 (ESV)
Give thanks in all circumstances; for this is
the will of God in Christ Jesus for you.

Self-pity is not what God wants us to feel. He wants to stand in a place of victory. A victor stands tall and faces the battles of life with his or her head held high. I pray that you allow God to strengthen the weak places in your life so that you will abandon the pity party and emerge victorious!

_____

_____

_____

_____

_____

_____

_____

_____

_____

June

I will seek peace with my neighbor.

MARK 12:31 (NIV)
The second is this: "Love your neighbor as yourself."
There is no commandment greater than these.

Have you recently had a disagreement in your life?
God calls for us to make peace when we have an
ought with people in our life. I challenge you to
make the first move and contact that person to
make amends. Who will you reach out to today?

_____

_____

_____

_____

_____

_____

_____

_____

I will love people who are hard to love.

JOHN 5:12
This is my commandment, that you love
one another as I have loved.

It's easy to love someone who is bubbly, kind, and sweet.
But what about the person who always has a bad attitude?
Or the person who never has anything nice to say? God
wants us to love them too. It's not easy, but it is God's will.
What unlovable person in your life will you love today?

_____

_____

_____

_____

_____

_____

_____

_____

I will stop what I'm doing right now and take
five minutes to praise and worship.

PSALM 150:6 (ESV)
Let everything that has breath praise
the Lord! Praise the Lord!

Praise him for your health, your family, your job,
your vehicle, your home, your friends, your food,
etc. This list could be 1,000 pages long, and we still
couldn't praise and thank him enough for all that he
has done! Give God five minutes of crazy praise!

JUNE 4

I will expect God to show up in his time and in his way.

Proverbs 3:5-6

Trust in the Lord with all your heart, and do not lean on your own understanding. In all your ways acknowledge him, and he will make straight your paths.

Accepting that God's timing is not ours is an act of trust. When we try to "help him out," we make a mess of things. Let God be God in your life. Believe that he will help you and expect him. Know that he is always on time and there are no messes when he is involved.

___

___

___

___

___

___

___

I will breathe and let it go.

1 PETER 5:7
Cast all your anxieties on him, because he cares for you.

God wants you to put your energy in trusting him. Don't allow life to cause you to be anxious or unsure. Trust and believe that God is in control, despite how things look. Take a deep breath and enjoy the rest of your day! God's got it!

_____

_____

_____

_____

_____

_____

_____

_____

_____

_____

JUNE 6

I will believe what I cannot see.

2 CORINTHIANS 5:7 (NIV)
For we live by faith, not by sight.

Have you been struggling in your faith lately? You are not alone. Believing what you cannot see is difficult! As you continually see God work on your behalf, your faith will start to increase. It all starts with your belief in him.

_____

_____

_____

_____

_____

_____

_____

_____

_____

_____

I will not be dishonest with myself.

JOHN 8:32 (NLT)
And you will know the truth, and the truth will set you free.

God calls us to walk in honesty in all aspects of our lives. Don't be afraid of your personal truth. In being truthful with ourselves, we can begin the path to healing. What will you be honest with yourself about today?

I will put my relationship with God
at the forefront of my life.

JOHN 15:5 (ESV)
I am the vine; you are the branches. Whoever
abides in me and I in him, he it is that bears much
fruit, for apart from me you can do nothing.

Is God the head of your life? If not, what is? God
wants us to live for him. He created us to live for
him. Allow him to take the proper place in your
life, and watch things change for the better!

I will not participate in bringing shame to my family.

EPHESIANS 6:2 (HCSB)
Honor your father and mother, which is the
first commandment with a promise.

Our relationships with family members are our first
introductions to love. We can't choose our family
because God chose them for us before the foundation
of the world. The people who love you are affected
by your actions. Be sure that you are always acting
in a way that will bring them honor, not shame.

I will always seek the truth.

JOHN 17:17 (ESV)
Sanctify them in the truth; your word is the truth.

God is not present where there is a lack of truth. He wants us to seek the truth in all situations. We can find truth in his word. Will you seek his word for truth today?

_____

_____

_____

_____

_____

_____

_____

_____

_____

_____

JUNE 11

I will strive to be my brother and sister's keeper.

ROMANS 12:10 (NKJV)
Be kindly affectionate to one another with brotherly
love, in honor giving preference to one another.

We are brothers and sisters in the Body of Christ. God
has called us to care for one another as such. How
can you be there for your brother and sister today?

_____

_____

_____

_____

_____

_____

_____

_____

_____

I will trust God to do what I see as impossible.

MATTHEW 19:26 (NIV)
Jesus looked at them and said, "With man this is impossible, but with God all things are possible."

Do you believe that God is able to do the impossible? His word is full of stories of him turning the impossible into reality. What impossible possibility are you believing God for today?

_____

_____

_____

_____

_____

_____

_____

_____

_____

I will set big goals and execute them.

2 CHRONICLES 15:7
But as for you, be strong and do not give
up, for your work will be rewarded.

God loves when we achieve our goals. He loves getting
behind our efforts and he wants to help us succeed. What
goals have you set today? What steps will you take to
execute them? God can't wait to celebrate your success!

_____

_____

_____

_____

_____

_____

_____

_____

_____

JUNE 14

I will always take the high road.

PSALM 15:1-2

Lord, who may dwell in your sacred tent? Who
may live on your holy mountain? The one whose
walk is blameless, who does what is righteous,
who speaks the truth from their heart.

Michelle Obama made headlines for this quote during
her speech at the Democratic National Convention:
"When they go low, we go high." Truly, there are few more
important calls that God has for us. To be Christ like, we
must always operate with the utmost grace in the most
trying situations. So the next time you are in traffic and
someone does a certain gesture in a fit of road rage,
resist the urge to do the same. Instead, flash them your
winning smile and keep it moving! Have a fantastic day!

JUNE 15

I will walk in my God-given authority.

LUKE 10:19 (NKJV)
Behold, I give you the authority to trample on
serpents and scorpions, and over all the power of the
enemy, and nothing shall by any means hurt you.

When you have authority over something, it has no
power to overcome you. This is true in every arena
of your life because you are a child of the King!
Walk in his authority today! God loves you!

_____

_____

_____

_____

_____

_____

_____

_____

My family will always come first.

1 Timothy 5:8 (NIV)
Anyone who does not provide for their relatives,
and especially for their own household, has denied
the faith and is worse than an unbeliever.

God loves family. He wants us to always make them
the top priority in our lives. Nothing matters more
than those you are blessed to call your family. Have
you been putting other things before your family?

_____

_____

_____

_____

_____

_____

_____

_____

JUNE 17

I will not lower my standards to fit in with
a group of people who have none.

ROMANS 12:9 (NASB)
Let love be without hypocrisy. Abhor
what is evil; cling to what is good.

Have you felt pressure to fit in with your peers lately?
It is normal and natural for us to want to be accepted
by others. However, God calls us, his children, to a
certain standard. If you find yourself in a group of people
who do not share that same standard, don't change
to fit in with them. In fact, seek to bring them up to
the standard that is Christ by witnessing to them.

I will stop holding grudges.

LEVITICUS 19:18
You shall not take vengeance, nor bear any grudge
against the sons of your people, but you shall love
your neighbor as yourself; I am the Lord.

Still mad at the kid who cut you in the lunch line
back in middle school? When someone has wronged
or hurt us, it is easy to feel mad at them. However,
holding a grudge actually requires more emotional
energy than forgiving them. I know it is not easy, but
start on the path of forgiving that person today.

_____

_____

_____

_____

_____

_____

_____

I will never accept being less than
who God expects me to be.

LUKE 15:11-17 (NIV)
(The entire story extends to verse 32.)
The Story of the Prodigal Son

Jesus continued: There was a man who had two sons. The younger one said to his father, "Father, give me my share of the estate." So he divided his property between them. Not long after that, the younger son got together all he had, set off for a distant country and there squandered his wealth in wild living. After he had spent everything, there was a severe famine in that whole country, and he began to be in need. So he went and hired himself out to a citizen of that country, who sent him to his fields to feed pigs. He longed to fill his stomach with the pods that the pigs were eating, but no one gave him anything. When he came to his senses, he said, "How many of my father's hired servants have food to spare, and here I am starving to death!"

When we accept less than what God has for us, we are much like the prodigal son who was heir to a vast kingdom, yet found himself eating with pigs. Realize that you, too, are heir to a vast kingdom. God never intended for you live in lack. Walk in your heritage!

I will not miss out on fulfilling God's purpose.

ROMANS 8:30 (NASB)
And these whom He predestined, He also called;
and these whom He called, He also justified; and
these whom He justified, He also glorified.

What is God's purpose for you? Are you walking
in that purpose? God yearns for us to live out the
vision that he has for our lives. What steps will
you take to live out God's purpose in your life?

_____

_____

_____

_____

_____

_____

_____

_____

JUNE 21

Today is the last day I will be broke.

MALACHI 3:10 (NIV)
Bring the whole tithe into the storehouse, that there
may be food in my house. Test me in this, says the
Lord Almighty, and see if I will not throw open the
floodgates of heaven and pour out so much blessing
that there will not be room enough to store it.

Do you believe that God wants you to prosper in every area
of your life? This includes your finances! If you are living
in lack today, I challenge you to seek out ways to make a
change in your life. No matter how big the mountain of your
finances may seem, nothing is too hard for God! Do you
trust that he has great financial blessings in store for you?

_____

_____

_____

_____

_____

_____

I will no longer allow people to leave me
feeling emotionally bankrupt.

Psalm 37:1-2 (NKJV)

Do not fret because of evildoers, Nor be envious of
the workers of iniquity. For they shall soon be cut
down like the grass, And wither as the green herb.

Have you ever felt emotionally drained after a
conversation with a particular person? Take note
of this and do your best to limit your interactions
with that person. God wants you to be uplifted by
someone's conversation and presence, not vice versa!

_____

_____

_____

_____

_____

_____

_____

I will not be involved in conversations
that do not bring glory to God.

PROVERBS 4:24
Keep your mouth free of perversity; keep
corrupt talk far from your lips.

As the Body of Christ, we are called to honor God
with the things we do and the things we say. Remove
yourself from any conversations that are not in
alignment with the things that please God.

I will be mindful of God's presence.

2 TIMOTHY 1:4 (KJV)
Greatly desiring to see thee, being mindful of
thy tears, that I may be filled with joy.

When we are fully aware of God's presence in our lives,
everything changes. It's just like turning on a light switch
when you enter a room. Suddenly, everything becomes
visible and bright. God's presence is the same way.
Turn on the light of God's presence in your life today.

_____

_____

_____

_____

_____

_____

_____

_____

I will encourage myself today.

PSALM 23:4 (ESV)
Even though I walk through the valley of the
shadow of death, I will fear no evil, for you are with
me; your rod and your staff, they comfort me.

No one knows what lifts your spirits better than you.
Life gets tough, and we all get down from time to time.
However, on this day, I challenge you to encourage
yourself! Think yourself happy! Dwell on God's love for
you! You will be surprised at how your mood will change
after you have spent some time uplifting yourself.

I will frequently remind myself that I deserve the best.

ROMANS 4:13 (NASB)
For the promise to Abraham or to his descendants
that he would be heir of the world was not through
the law, but through the righteousness of faith.

We are the seed of Abraham. We are God's chosen
people. We deserve the best! The best of everything.
God wants you to know that and remember it always.
If your current situation does not reflect what you
deserve, continue to go before God and watch him
work! You are the best and you deserve the best!

I will pray for my family intentionally every day.

1 Chronicles 16:11 (NIV)
Look to the Lord and his strength; seek his face always.

Are you intentional and specific when you pray? I challenge you to try writing your prayers today. Make them intentional and highly specific pertaining to the goals that you have for your family. Tell God exactly what you need and want him to do for your family. Share your prayer with your family and set some quiet time to discuss together.

I will share my dreams with the people
God directs me to share them with.

JOB 33:15 (NLV)
He speaks in dreams, in visions of the night, when
deep sleep falls on people as they lie in their beds.

God instructs us through his word. Has he recently
instructed you to share a dream with someone?
Maybe he placed them on your heart during
prayer yesterday. Be obedient to that instruction.
There are always reasons bigger than us behind
God's direction. Have an amazing day today!

I will expect God to supply my needs.

PHILIPPIANS 4:19 (KJV)
But my God shall supply all your needs according
to his riches in glory by Christ Jesus.

Do you believe that God can and will supply your
needs? Do you trust him with the matters of your life?
God longs for our trust in him. When we place him
first in our lives, he is in position to supply all that we
could ask. Rest in this truth today. God loves you!

JUNE 30

I will be in radical pursuit of my goals.

PROVERBS 42:27 (NIV)
Put your outdoor work in order and get your
fields ready; after that build your house.

Have you lost the fire in the pursuit of your goals and
dreams? Ask God to reignite that flame. You can do
amazing things when you are motivated and inspired
to do so! You are unstoppable! Walk in this today.

July

JULY 1

I will not allow negative thoughts to
linger throughout this day.

PHILIPPIANS 2:1-2

Therefore if you have any encouragement from being united
with Christ, if any comfort from his love, if any common
sharing in the Spirit, if any tenderness and compassion,
then make my joy complete by being like-minded, having
the same love, being one in spirit and of one mind.

Have you ever had one of those mornings when you
think to yourself "today is not going to be a good day for
me"? We all have. If today started that way, I challenge
you to put a stop to the negative thoughts right now.
Today will be a great day, and you will not allow the
inconveniences that started your day to dictate your
day. This is that "redo" button that you need. God loves
you. He woke you up this morning—praise him!

_____

_____

_____

_____

I will be everything that I aspire to be.

PROVERBS 16:3 (ESV)
Commit your work to the Lord, and
your plans will be established.

Do you remember as a child, adults often asked, "What do you want to be when you grow up?" What did you answer when asked that question? Chances are, the answer has changed a few times. Are you running after the person you want to be? If not, what can you do to change that today? Walk in greatness today!

_____

_____

_____

_____

_____

_____

_____

I am willing to do the necessary work to make my life better.

JOHN 16:33

I have said these things to you, that in me you may have peace. In the world you will have tribulation. But take heart; I have overcome the world.

What areas are lacking in your life? What things require God's attention the most? Trust that God will give you the strength you need to make your life amazing. He wants you to live a life that you love. Are you willing to work toward that goal?

_____

_____

_____

_____

_____

_____

_____

_____

I am an independent thinker.

1 PETER 2:16
Live as people who are free, not using your freedom
as a cover-up for evil, but living as servants of God.

Do you allow societal norms and popular culture to
decide things for you? At some point, we all have or
will. God wants us to think for ourselves, of course
in accordance with his will and his word. Don't fall
victim to "monkey see, monkey do" mentality. Follow
God's word and be your own man or woman.

_____

_____

_____

_____

_____

_____

_____

_____

I will be a rainbow on someone's cloudy day.

1 PETER 4:13 (NIV)
But rejoice inasmuch as you participate in
the sufferings of Christ, so that you may be
overjoyed when his glory is revealed.

God's heart hurts when we hurt. What better way to show
the love of God to someone than to cheer them up with a
kind word or action? Whose day will you brighten today?

_____

_____

_____

_____

_____

_____

_____

_____

I will always give my best to my family.

1 PETER 4:8
Above all, love each other deeply, because
love covers a multitude of sins.

"If you want to change the world, go
home and love your family."
–Mother Theresa

Family is one of God's greatest gifts to us. The foundation
of life is the familial bond. How can you give your best
to your family? Put them before anything and everyone.
Listen when they talk to you. Anticipate their needs.
Pray for them. Most of all, love them unconditionally.

_____

_____

_____

_____

_____

_____

_____

I will stop being a doormat.

DEUTERONOMY 28:13
The Lord will make you the head, not the tail. If you
pay attention to the commands of the Lord your God
that I give you this day and carefully follow them,
you will always be at the top, never the bottom.

Are you allowing someone to use you? Do you fail
to speak up for yourself because you are afraid of
the consequences? God has called us to be mighty
in his name. Know that God thinks highly of you.
Never be afraid to stand up for yourself!

JULY 8

I will break all cycles of abuse in my life.
–Alexandria L. Barlowe

ISAIAH 41:10
So do not fear, for I am with you; do not be dismayed,
for I am your God. I will strengthen you and help you;
I will uphold you with my righteous right hand.

God is not pleased when his children are mistreated. Are
you stuck in an abusive relationship? Do you feel like you
can't get out? God always has a way out of the wilderness. I
stand in prayer with you right now that a way of escape be
made clear to you. You are loved. You are worthy of God's
help and you are enough. This is not the end of you. You
will have the victory in this situation, in the name of Jesus!

_____

_____

_____

_____

_____

_____

I will rest well tonight knowing that God is in control.

MATTHEW 11:28
Come to me, all you who are weary and
burdened, and I will give you rest.

Is there a situation in your life that has you feeling
heavily burdened? Chances are if you are a human being,
the answer is yes. We all feel burdened by something
in our lives, but we are truly fortunate to serve a God
who can handle our burdens. I challenge you to stop
worrying and completely surrender your situation to
God. Let him fight your battles and get some rest!

JULY 10

I will mind my own business.

1 Thessalonians 4:11-12 (ESV)
And to aspire to live quietly, and to mind your
own affairs, and to work with your hands, as we
instructed you, so that you may walk properly
before outsiders and be dependent on no one.

Do you remember being told this as a child? I can still
hear my mother telling me to keep my nose out of other
people's business. These are words of wisdom and only for
our benefit. You can't fully focus on being the best version
of yourself if you are always preoccupied with what is
going on with everyone around you. Ask God to help you
to be focused on your goals and plans. Enjoy being you!

I will regard humility as an asset.

PROVERBS 11:2 (NIV)
When pride comes, then comes disgrace,
but with humility comes wisdom.

God causes us to act with humility in everything
we do. When we put the needs of others before our
own, we are truly embodying what it means to be
like Him. How will you practice humility today?

_____

_____

_____

_____

_____

_____

_____

_____

_____

_____

I will no longer participate in activities
that do not please God.

1 PETER 4:15 (ESV)
But let none of you suffer as a murderer or
a thief or an evildoer or as a meddler.

Are you struggling to cease actions that do not bring
honor to God? You are not alone. God loves you. He
wants you to walk in righteousness. He understands your
thoughts and your feelings. He knows that you want to
change. Ask him to help you. Invite him into your heart
and home. I pray in agreement with you for complete and
total deliverance, no condemnation necessary. I believe
in you. God believes in you. Do you believe in you?

I will have the courage to correct my
brothers and sisters in love.

PSALM 94:12 (NASB)
Blessed is the man whom You chasten, O Lord,
and whom you teach out of your law.

Correcting someone when they are wrong is a good thing.
Often, we place a negative connotation on giving and
receiving correction. When we are gently and lovingly
redirected, we are given a chance to do something
the right way. Be sure to correct in love and know
that you are helping the person you are correcting.

I will forgive myself as often as I need to.

2 CORINTHIANS 5:17 (NIV)
Therefore, if anyone is in Christ, the new creation
has come: The old has gone, the new is here!

God is a God of forgiveness. No one is perfect
and we all fall sometimes. It's not the fall that is
important, it is the getting up! Forgive yourself
when you fall short. Let your disappointment fuel
your determination to get to your destiny.

_____

_____

_____

_____

_____

_____

_____

_____

I choose to live my dreams.

PSALM 33:11
But the plans of the Lord stand firm forever, the
purposes of his heart through all generations.

What is your dream? What would you do if you knew
you could not fail? The answers to these questions
unlock our passions and the essence of who we are. I
challenge you to choose you today. If you are working
at a job that you are not passionate about, I challenge
you to begin your exit strategy. Life is short, and
tomorrow is not promised. We owe it to ourselves
and to our heavenly Father who loves us to live a life
that we love. Will you choose to live your dreams?

_____

_____

_____

_____

_____

_____

JULY 16

I will never doubt myself again.

PHILIPPIANS 1:6 (NKJV)
Being confident of this very thing, that He who has begun a good work in you will perfect it until the day of Jesus Christ.

Confidence is key! Do you know who you belong to? You are a child of the King! You are truly amazing! God loves you! He created you in his image. He hurts when we doubt ourselves because we are essentially telling him, "I don't like what you made." Love yourself and know that you are capable! You can do whatever you set your mind to. You can be the person you want to be. Are you willing to embrace the possibilities that arise when you are confident in yourself?

I will not concern myself with what people
say and feel about my dreams.

DEUTERONOMY 31:6 (NASB)
Be strong and courageous, do not be afraid or tremble
at them, for the Lord your God is the one who goes
with you He will not fail you or forsake you.

Have you recently become discouraged because of the
opinions and comments of others? Know that God gave
you your dream when he created you. He wants you
to seek his approval, not that of others. As long as you
have his stamp of approval, you need nothing more.

I will use what God has already provided.

MATTHEW 6:26

Look at the birds of the air, that they do not sow, nor reap nor gather into barns, and yet your heavenly Father feeds them. Are you not worth much more than they?

What are the tools that God has given you? When we are resourceful with God's gifts, we are showing him that we are grateful for his blessings. We often pray for increase. There is nothing wrong with increase, but are you making good use of what you currently have in your tool belt? What will you make excellent use of today? Be blessed!

_____

_____

_____

_____

_____

_____

_____

I will stop competing and comparing myself with others.

JAMES 3:16 (ESV)
For where jealousy and selfish ambition exist,
there will be disorder and every vile practice.

Have you ever heard the expression, "run your own race"? Think about being in the 100-meter dash in track and field. If you are constantly looking over in the lanes beside you, you will undoubtedly start to drift into a competitor's lane. In the sport, you are automatically disqualified if you step out of your lane. This is a powerful way to look at your life. How can you remain focused on your own life if you are constantly looking in someone else's lane? Will you make a promise to yourself that you will stay focused on your own race today?

_____

_____

_____

_____

_____

_____

I will have an amazing day today.

PHILIPPIANS 4:4 (NASB)
Rejoice in the Lord always; again I will say, rejoice!

You have breath in your body! You have health and
strength! You are alive and well! Since you are
reading this, I know that you will have an amazingly
spectacular day today. Frustrating things may happen
to you today, but they will not steal your joy! Why?
Because the very beat of your heart is reason enough
for you to have a great day today! God loves you!

_____

_____

_____

_____

_____

_____

_____

_____

I will be an active listener.

JAMES 1:22 (NIV)
Do not merely listen to the word, and so
deceive yourselves. Do what it says.

To be an active listener means to hear and participate in
what is being said. What other things come to mind when
you think about what it means to be an active listener? Do
you actively participate when having a conversation with a
peer or loved one? Do you actively participate when hearing
a word from God? I challenge you to practice being an
active listener in the conversations that you have today!

_____

_____

_____

_____

_____

_____

_____

I will seek out opportunities to develop myself.

EPHESIANS 6:11 (ESV)
Put on the whole armor of God, that you may be
able to stand against the schemes of the devil.

When we better ourselves, we honor God. We express
our appreciation for what he has given us by making
it better. What opportunities will you seek today? How
can you develop yourself? What skills will you sharpen
with practice and dedication? You are amazing and
you will do great things. Walk in your greatness.

_____

_____

_____

_____

_____

_____

_____

_____

I will deliver what I promise.

NUMBERS 30:2
If a man vows a vow to the Lord, or swears an oath to
bind himself by a pledge, he shall not break his word. He
shall do according to all that proceeds out of his mouth.

Being a man or woman of your word is one of the
many ways that you can be Christ like. Have you
ever had someone drop their end of a bargain or
promise that they made to you? How did their actions
make you feel? God calls us to a higher standard.
What promises will you deliver on today?

_____

_____

_____

_____

_____

_____

I will respect the opinions of others
even if they differ from mine.

ROMANS 14:1 (NASB)
Now accept the one who is weak in faith, but not for
the purpose of passing judgment on his opinions.

We are all entitled to our opinions and points of view.
We should respect the opinions of others even if they
differ from our own. Chances are you know several
people who have opinions that differ from your own. I
challenge you to embrace the variety of views within
your inner circle. How will you react and respond the
next time you are in a conversation with someone
who has an opinion in stark contrast to your own?

My life and space are a gossip-free zone.

PSALM 141:3
Set a guard, O Lord, over my mouth; keep
watch over the door of my lips.

It can be tempting to get involved in gossip, but God is
not pleased with this type of conversation. I challenge
you to pray for someone who is the topic of gossip
within your inner circle. Do your part to positively
influence friends against gossiping about others.

I will build someone's confidence with my words today.

ROMANS 14:19 (ESV)
So then let us pursue what makes for
peace and for mutual upbuilding.

How can you uplift someone's confidence today? What can you say to someone you know that will enhance their self-esteem? A genuine, kind word costs absolutely nothing to say, but it can go a long way in making someone feel better.

_____

_____

_____

_____

_____

_____

_____

_____

_____

I will place my family ahead of my career.

PROVERBS 15:27 (NIV)
The greedy bring ruin to their households,
but the one who hates bribes will live.

Your career is important and a blessing from God, but it should not take priority over your family. What are some ways that you can achieve a healthy work-life balance? Can you arrange your work schedule to ensure that you are available for sports practices and games, recitals, and programs? It may require some extra planning and effort, but your family is worth it. Will you commit to making your family your first priority today?

_____

_____

_____

_____

_____

_____

_____

I will not return evil with evil.

1 PETER 3:9

Do not repay evil with evil or insult with insult. On the contrary, repay evil with blessing, because to this you were called so that you may inherit a blessing.

Have you noticed a theme within the character of God? He embodies what it means to be kind and not spiteful. Have you ever felt vengeful toward someone? Did you act on those feelings? I challenge you to resist the desire to get revenge when you have been wronged. Remind yourself that God fights your battles for you. He always has the last word.

I will love myself even when I feel unlovable.

ROMANS 3:23
For all have sinned and fall short of the glory of God.

Do you know how much you mean to God? Do you know how much he loves you? He absolutely adores you and he never feels like you are unlovable. You may feel that way, but he does not. God understands our shortcomings and he does not hold them against us. I challenge you to remind yourself daily of God's love for you. I pray that you accept his love for you in the times when you need it the most.

_____

_____

_____

_____

_____

_____

_____

I will be slow to anger and quick to forgive.

JAMES 1:19 (NKJV)
So then, my beloved brethren, let every man be swift
to hear, slow to speak, slow to wrath; for the wrath of
man does not produce the righteousness of God.

God epitomizes grace and forgiveness. Tackling our
emotions can prove to be challenging, especially when
someone has done something to make us angry. God calls
us to a higher standard. It takes a great deal of self-control
and patience to forgive when you have been wronged.
I pray in agreement with you for God's peace the next
time you find yourself becoming angry for any reason.

I will seek joy because happiness is fleeting.

PSALM 47:1 (NIV)
Clap your hands, all you nations; shout
to God with cries of joy.

What does joy mean to you? What things bring you joy?
True joy doesn't require a reason, it just is. Happiness is
conditional while joy is free of stipulations. Do you believe
God can clothe you in joy regardless of your situation?

_____

_____

_____

_____

_____

_____

_____

_____

_____

August

I will stop replacing relationship with religion.
–Alexandria L. Barlowe

JOHN 14:6 (ESV)
Jesus said to him, "I am the way, and the truth, and the life. No one comes to the Father except through me."

A relationship with God is not contingent upon rituals, church attendance, or social status. Do you talk to God every day? Do you seek to know his character? Do you spend time in his presence? Do you live as his word instructs you to? These are some things to consider in your relationship with God. Are you in religion or in relationship with God?

I will stop wishing for someone else's
life and live my own, mindfully.

PROVERBS 14:30
A tranquil heart gives life to the flesh,
but envy makes the bones rot.

Envy and jealousy can creep up on you when you perceive
that someone has an advantage or advantages that you
do not have or have access to. When we feel this way, we
negate the power of God in our lives. God has enough
blessings for everyone. What is for you, is for you—it
has nothing to do with what your peers have. Do you
trust that you have no need to be jealous of your peers
because God has something special set aside for you?

I will not allow complainers to occupy my time.

PHILIPPIANS 2:14
Do all things without grumbling or disputing.

When we complain, we give our problems more power than they deserve. Being around someone who complains can zap positive energy quickly. If you can help it, try to be around people who are more focused on finding a solution as opposed to complaining about what is wrong. How can you lovingly redirect someone who is a chronic complainer?

_____

_____

_____

_____

_____

_____

_____

I will not dumb down my gifts to make
others feel comfortable.

ACTS 1:8 (NASB)
But you will receive power when the Holy Spirit
has come upon you; and you shall be My witnesses
both in Jerusalem, and in all Judea and Samaria,
and even to the remotest part of the earth.

Dulling your shine won't make someone else's light
shine any brighter. Don't feel like you need to change
in any way for anyone. God blessed you with your gifts
for the world to see. Let them shine bright always!
You are a stellar human being. Walk in this today!

I will rest in the Lord.

PSALM 37:7

Rest in the Lord and wait patiently for Him; do not
fret because of him who prospers in his way, because
of the man who carries out wicked schemes.

What does resting in the Lord mean to you? Do you
trust God and believe that he is a fair and just God?
When we rely completely on him to supply our needs,
we can rest in him. He wants to do our heavy lifting
and loves providing for us. Will you rest in him?

_____

_____

_____

_____

_____

_____

_____

_____

AUGUST 6

I will stop seeking acceptance and approval from man.

GALATIANS 1:10 (ESV)
For am I now seeking the approval of man, or of God?
Or am I trying to please man? If I were still trying to
please man, I would not be a servant of Christ.

God made us to want to relate to and connect with other
people. He understands the human psyche and our need
for acceptance and approval, but he wants us to look to
him for it. Will you shift your focus from pleasing man
to pleasing God? What does this look like in your life?

_____

_____

_____

_____

_____

_____

_____

_____

I am determined to live my purpose.

PSALM 138:8
The Lord will fulfill his purpose for me; your
steadfast love, O Lord, endures forever. Do
not forsake the work of your hands.

What is your purpose? What has God called you to do?
Who has he called you to be? Are you currently living out
that purpose? What is keeping you from fulfilling your
God-given purpose? I challenge you to do one thing that
will get you one step closer to fulfilling your purpose today.

_____

_____

_____

_____

_____

_____

_____

_____

I will exercise three to five times per week.

1 CORINTHIANS 9:27
But I discipline my body and keep it under control, lest after preaching to others I myself should be disqualified.

Maintaining our physical health is important to God. He has given us our bodies while here on Earth, and we should do all that we can to properly care for it. When we exercise, our bodies perform optimally. Consequently, we feel and look better. Will you work out today?

_____

_____

_____

_____

_____

_____

_____

_____

I will live for Jesus Christ.

MATTHEW 6:24

No one can serve two masters, for either he will hate the one and love the other, or he will be devoted to the one and despise the other. You cannot serve God and money.

What does living for Jesus mean to you? Are you currently living for him? His word reveals the things necessary to live for him. I challenge you to tap into the resource of his word today.

I believe God hears my cries.

REVELATION 21:4 (NASB)
And He will wipe away every tear from their
eyes; and there will no longer be any death;
there will no longer be any mourning, or crying,
or pain; the first things have passed away.

You are never alone when you are a child of the King. Some experiences may cause you to feel isolated, but he is always with you. He sees you, he hears you, and he loves you. God carries us through our darkest times and is a great healer of broken hearts. Don't ever doubt that he is listening.

I will turn love into an action word in my life.

1 CORINTHIANS 13:4-8 (NIV)
Love is patient, love is kind. It does not envy, it does not boast, it is not proud. It does not dishonor others, it is not self-seeking, it is not easily angered, it keeps no record of wrongs. Love does not delight in evil but rejoices with the truth. It always protects, always trusts, always hopes, always perseveres. Love never fails. But where there are prophecies, they will cease; where there are tongues, they will be stilled; where there is knowledge, it will pass away.

What does love mean to you? Is love an action word in your life? Do you seek to do everything in love? Love is the greatest commandment that God gives us. How can you exemplify love in every aspect of your life? How will you spread love today?

_____

_____

_____

_____

_____

AUGUST 12

I will collaborate with and complement others.

MATTHEW 18:20
For where two or three gather in my
name, there am I with them.

God loves when we work with others. How do you
collaborate with others in your professional life?
In your personal life? In your church community?
Do you complement others with what you bring
to the table? I challenge you to get involved with a
project that allows you to work alongside others to
achieve a goal. Teamwork makes dreams work.

_____

_____

_____

_____

_____

_____

_____

AUGUST 13

I will think thoughts of increase and abundance.

1 CHRONICLES 4:10
Jabez cried out to the God of Israel, "Oh, that you
would bless me and enlarge my territory! Let your
hand be with me, and keep me from harm so that I will
be free from pain." And God granted his request.

God wants to increase you! He wants to bless you with
more so that you can do more. He is a God of abundance
and he wants your life to be abundant in blessings, in
love, and in joy. Think of increase beyond monetary
and material things. Increase in every area is much
richer than money. Do you believe that increase is for
you? What things are in need of increase in your life?

_____

_____

_____

_____

_____

_____

I will not participate or facilitate in the
destruction of anyone's character.

PROVERBS 20:3 (ESV)
It is an honor for a man to keep aloof from
strife, but every fool will be quarreling.

God calls us to walk in peace and be free of strife.
If you are aware of or around actions or words that
could potentially be damaging to someone, do not
participate. God wants us to be a blessing to others
and build them up, not tear them down. Will you
be a difference maker when faced with this type of
situation? Will you seek to positively influence negative
behavior? I challenge you to be an agent for change!

_____

_____

_____

_____

_____

_____

I will walk in what God is calling me to do.

EPHESIANS 4:1 (NASB)
Therefore I, the prisoner of the Lord, implore
you to walk in a manner worthy of the calling
with which you have been called.

What has God called you to do? What has he placed on
your heart? Are you currently walking in that calling?
What is keeping you from doing so? I challenge you to
discover God's calling on your life and walk in it boldly.

_____

_____

_____

_____

_____

_____

_____

_____

I will not be jealous of anyone's life
or God's provision for them.

JAMES 3:14 (NIV)
But if you harbor bitter envy and selfish ambition in
your hearts, do not boast about it or deny the truth.

Have you been envying a friend or family member's
lifestyle? Do you feel as if they are more blessed than
you are? God doesn't want us to be jealous of anyone. Be
more focused on making the changes you want to see
in your life than what you see in someone else's. God
loves you and he has blessings that are specifically for
you. Do you believe in God's provision for your life?

_____

_____

_____

_____

_____

_____

_____

_____

I will find beauty in everything.

ECCLESIASTES 3:11
He has made everything beautiful in its time. He has
also set eternity in the human heart; yet no one can
fathom what God has done from beginning to end.

Finding beauty in challenging situations is certainly
not easy. It requires faith, which is necessary to please
God. When you have faith that God is working things
in your favor, regardless of how it looks, you will find
the beauty in even the ugliest situations. What specific
thing or situation will you find beauty in today?

_____

_____

_____

_____

_____

_____

_____

I will guard my heart from things that are unlike God.

PROVERBS 4:23 (ESV)
Keep your heart with all vigilance, for
from it flow the springs of life.

Your heart is the essence of who you are. That is why
it must be safely guarded and protected from unclean
things. Who do you need to guard your heart from?
What do you need to guard your heart from?

_____

_____

_____

_____

_____

_____

_____

_____

_____

I will not allow ignorance to harden my heart.

LUKE 23:34 (NIV)
Jesus said, "Father, forgive them, for they
do not know what they are doing." And they
divided up his clothes by casting lots.

To be ignorant means to be uninformed about a specific
subject or topic. One of the ways that ignorance manifests
itself is through prejudice. If you have experienced any
type of prejudice in any form, it can be hurtful, confusing,
and altogether disheartening. Although challenging,
don't allow this type of behavior to cause you to feel
bitter. God loves people of all colors, creeds, and walks
of life. Man may have prejudices, but he does not.

I will work on my purpose diligently.

PROVERBS 21:5 (NASB)
The plans of the diligent lead surely to advantage, but
everyone who is hasty comes surely to poverty.

What is your purpose? What actions do you need to
take in order to fulfill it? Are you working toward it
actively each and every day? What can you do today
to ensure that your purpose comes to fruition? I
challenge you to be bold and become intentional
in your pursuit of fulfilling your purpose.

I will not allow anyone to steal my peace.

COLOSSIANS 3:15 (NIV)
Let the peace of Christ rule in your hearts,
since as members of one body you were
called to peace. And be thankful.

What does peace mean to you? What things cause you to
feel at peace? Is there someone or something in your life
that causes your peace to slip away like a thief in the night?
Be mindful of things that disturb your personal peace.
Take complete ownership of ensuring that your heart,
mind, and home are peaceful. This means eradicating
your life of anything that is a threat to your peace.

I will raise children who do not have to
recover from their childhood.

EPHESIANS 6:4 (ESV)
Fathers, do not provoke your children to anger, but bring
them up in the discipline and instruction of the Lord.

Children are one of the greatest gifts that God gives us.
Raising them comes with a great deal of responsibility,
especially when it comes to their emotional well-being.
When it comes to parenting, we have to be true prayer
warriors. We have to be equipped with wisdom and
constantly seek God for guidance on how to tackle the
daily duties of raising little people. The most important
things you can do for your children are love them
and spend time with them. Start there—consistently
lift them up in prayer and let God do the rest.

_____

_____

_____

_____

_____

_____

I will teach people how to treat me by how I treat myself.

JOHN 15:12 (ESV)
This is my commandment, that you love
one another as I have loved you.

People take their cues on how to treat you from you!
What you allow will continue. Be sure that you are good
to yourself so that others will know what you will and will
not accept. Be good to yourself, and others will follow!

_____

_____

_____

_____

_____

_____

_____

_____

_____

I will not allow anyone to speak harshly toward me.

PROVERBS 12:18
There is one whose rash words are like sword thrusts, but the tongue of the wise brings healing.

"Sticks and stones may break my bones but words will never hurt me." Have you ever heard this saying? Unfortunately, this is not true! Words do hurt. They can cut deeper than we can see on the surface. Are there people in your life who do not speak to you peaceably? Correct them in love and lead by example. If you are not able to redirect their behavior, they do not need to be part of your life.

_____

_____

_____

_____

_____

_____

_____

I will be a voice for the voiceless.

ACTS 20:35

In all things I have shown you that by working hard in this way we must help the weak and remember the words of the Lord Jesus, how he himself said, "it is more blessed to give than to receive."

Are there people around you who are unable to speak up for themselves? Whether they be children, elderly, or suffering from a disability, we have a duty to ensure that they are heard and taken care of. How can you help them? Spend time with them and be an advocate for them when necessary and applicable.

_____

_____

_____

_____

_____

_____

AUGUST 26

I will stop trying to explain myself to people.

GENESIS 37:5 (NASB)
Then Joseph had a dream, and when he told it
to his brothers, they hated him even more.

You do not require any explanation for who you are! If
people do not understand you, that is okay! Although it
can be uncomfortable, it is okay to be misunderstood
by people because we are not misunderstood by God!

_____

_____

_____

_____

_____

_____

_____

_____

_____

I will not allow the negativity of
naysayers to seep into my spirit.

PSALM 3:1-2 (NKJV)

Lord, how they have increased who trouble me! Many
are they who rise up against me. Many are they who
say of me, "There is no help for him in God."

When God says yes, nobody can say no! It doesn't
matter who they are or what they mean to you, their no
is not stronger than God's yes. Don't be discouraged
by negativity. Don't allow anyone's words to deter
you or distract you from forward movement. God
always has the ultimate say, and he says YES!

I will praise God every time I feel like complaining.

EPHESIANS 5:20 (NASB)
Always giving thanks for all things in the name of
our Lord Jesus Christ to God, even the Father.

There is great power in turning a complaint into praise!
When we praise instead of complain, we are making
a distinct choice to choose to magnify God over our
problems. He is truly glorified when we choose to
praise him! Are you going to choose to praise today?

_____

_____

_____

_____

_____

_____

_____

_____

I will not let one incident dictate my entire day.

Romans 8:28 (NIV)
And we know that in all things God works
for the good of those who love him, who have
been called according to his purpose.

Have you ever had a morning that started in complete
and total chaos? Maybe the chaos made you feel on edge
and caused you to react in an unfavorable way. This
may have left you feeling like you wished you could hit a
"redo" button and start all over again. Let God be your
redo button. Your chaotic morning doesn't have to set the
tone for the rest of your day! Say this quick prayer: God,
please fix my attitude. Reset my tone this morning and
help me to be focused on you throughout the rest of this
day. In your name, I pray, Amen. Now, go enjoy your day!

I will persevere through difficult times and situations.

1 THESSALONIANS 5:16-18
Rejoice always, pray continually, give thanks in all circumstances; for this is God's will for you in Christ Jesus.

God does his best work during our night seasons. He teaches you and molds you when you feel you are at your lowest. Are you currently being faced with difficulty in your life? I want to encourage you of God's presence and strength during this time. He is with you! He will never leave you! He wants you to persevere and push through to the other side. You will survive this and be so much stronger and wiser. Stay strong. Keep your head up! Don't ever stop moving forward!

_____

_____

_____

_____

_____

_____

AUGUST 31

I am healed.

ISAIAH 53:5

But he was pierced for our transgressions, he was
crushed for our iniquities; the punishment that brought
us peace was on him, and by his wounds we are healed.

What a wonderful healer we serve! Isn't it a blessing
to know that he endured great pain and suffering for
us? I speak to each and every malady and ailment
that you may be facing right now. God said that you
were already healed. Speak your healing right now!
Claim it and it is yours! I am praying and standing in
agreement with you! You are healed in Jesus' name!

September

SEPTEMBER 1

I will be open to love after heartbreak.
–Alexandria L. Barlowe

PSALM 84:11 (NKJV)
For the Lord God is a sun and shield; The Lord
will give grace and glory; No good thing will He
withhold from those who walk uprightly.

Heartbreak is no easy obstacle to overcome. God loves
the broken hearted, and his specialty is healing broken
hearts. He wants to give you double for your trouble, and
I am a living witness that he can give you a happiness
so great that it causes you to forget your pain. Do you
believe? Will you leave your heart open for love again?

I will listen to understand instead of listening to respond.

PROVERBS 16:20
Whoever gives heed to instruction prospers, and
blessed is the one who trusts in the Lord.

When talking to others, do you listen and wholeheartedly
focus on what the other person is saying? Do you find
yourself interrupting them or rushing them to get to
the end of their story? These are signs that you may be
listening only to respond instead of listening to truly
understand. The next time you are having a conversation
with someone, I challenge you to focus on what they are
saying. Don't be worried about what you are going to
say in response. Concentrate on what they are saying.
Making the shift in your communication will make
for more effective conversation as well as enhance
your connection with the person you are talking to.

New contacts and contracts will find me today.

1 KINGS 2:3

And observe what the Lord your God requires:
Walk in obedience to him, and keep his decrees
and commands, his laws and regulations, as
written in the Law of Moses. Do this so that you
may prosper in all you do and wherever you go.

In the beginning phases of building your business, your
next paycheck is only as strong as your networking skills.
Finding new people to do business with is the key to
your success. This can be frustrating and sometimes
uncertain, but I am here to encourage you. You will be
successful in your business venture. You will find the
investors and the clients that you need. You will be a
magnet for excellent business deals, in Jesus' name! I
believe in you and I believe God! What do you believe?

_____

_____

_____

_____

_____

I will make better food choices than I did yesterday.

PROVERBS 3:7-8

Do not be wise in your own eyes; fear the Lord
and shun evil. This will bring health to your
body and nourishment to your bones.

Eating healthy is one of the greatest ways we can pay
ourselves. When we eat better, we feel better. It is so
important that we are conscious about what we put into
our bodies. Dieting is not the key to making good food
choices—lifestyle is. You do not have to deprive yourself
in order to make healthy food choices. There are healthy
alternatives for cravings, and portion control allows us to
enjoy the foods we love in moderation. Will you swap an
unhealthy meal or snack for a healthier alternative today?

I am wealthy.

PROVERBS 13:11
Dishonest money dwindles away, but whoever
gathers money little by little makes it grow.

Do you believe that God has great wealth in store for
you? He does not want his people to live in lack. Think
about it. If he called us to help and bless others, he
knows he has to provide us with the resources to do
so. God blesses us so that we can be a blessing. Believe
that wealth is for you and that it is coming! Do you
believe and receive God's plan for wealth in your life?

_____

_____

_____

_____

_____

_____

_____

SEPTEMBER 6

I will cast my burdens on God.

PSALM 55:22 (NHEB)
Cast your burden on the Lord, and he will sustain you; He will never allow the righteous to be moved.

God wants you to bring your cares to him. You can't handle them, but he can! He is always available for you. Do you take advantage of his strength and power? Do you try to do everything yourself as opposed to carrying your burdens to him? I challenge you to give your troubles to him and watch him work. He is ready and waiting for you to lean and depend on him. Will you?

I believe in me.

PSALM 3:4 (NKJV)
I cried to the Lord with my voice, and
He heard me from His holy hill.

Do you believe in your God-given abilities? Do you believe
that God has great things in store for your life? Do you
believe that good things will find you? Belief in yourself
is crucial to your success. God believes in you! He wants
you to believe in yourself and your dreams as well.

_____

_____

_____

_____

_____

_____

_____

_____

_____

I have been chosen for greatness.

MATTHEW 22:14 (ESV)
For many are called, but few are chosen.

To be part of God's chosen people is truly an honor. It also comes with a great deal of responsibility to carry out God's vision for your life. Do you believe that you are part of God's chosen few? Do you believe that you are destined for greatness?

_____

_____

_____

_____

_____

_____

_____

_____

_____

My life has meaning, purpose, and value.

JEREMIAH 1:5
Before I formed you in the womb I knew you,
and before you were born I consecrated you; I
appointed you a prophet to the nations.

God loves you so much. When he created you, he
instilled greatness into your DNA. You must believe
this. You matter. You are worthy of good things.
Your life is valuable! Regardless of what you have
been through, what you are going through, or how
you feel, you matter! Please don't ever forget it!

_____

_____

_____

_____

_____

_____

_____

I am an overcomer by faith.

1 JOHN 5:4 (NIV)

For everyone born of God overcomes the world. This is
the victory that has overcome the world, even our faith.

Our faith can stand in the gap for us when we need
it the most! With faith, you can truly overcome any
situation that you are faced with. How strong is your
faith? Do you believe that you have already overcome?

_____

_____

_____

_____

_____

_____

_____

_____

_____

My gift is unique.

EPHESIANS 2:10 (ESV)
For we are his workmanship, created in Christ
Jesus for good works, which God prepared
beforehand, that we should walk in them.

You are one of a kind. When God created you, he made
you like no other. Even if you are a twin, there is no other
person on Earth who is like you. This includes your
gifts and talents, too. There may be other people who
share similar gifts, but no one can do it quite like you.
Know that God broke the mold when he made you!

_____

_____

_____

_____

_____

_____

_____

I will stop destructive behaviors.

GALATIANS 5:19-21
Now the works of the flesh are evident: sexual immorality, impurity, sensuality, idolatry, sorcery, enmity, strife, jealousy, fits of anger, rivalries, dissensions, divisions, envy, drunkenness, orgies and things like these. I warn you, as I warned you before, that those who do such things will not inherit the kingdom of God.

God loves you more than your mind can fathom. Just as a loving parent provides guidance and structure for their children, God provides you guidelines with your best interest at heart. God wants us to live the abundant life, free of condemnation. Destructive behaviors hinder us from doing so. Will you rid your life of behaviors that do not benefit you?

I will seek out a mentor in my field.

2 TIMOTHY 2:2
And what you have heard from me in the
presence of many witnesses entrust to faithful
men, who will be able to teach others also.

When you want to accomplish something, it is wise to find
someone who is currently operating in that field. Someone
who has been where you are trying to go will be able to
give you valuable insight into the steps you need to take
to be successful. When you are reaching for greatness,
you need help along the way. Don't be afraid to seek it!

I will volunteer my time and skills to
someone who is in need.

GALATIANS 6:10
So then, as we have opportunity, let us do good to everyone,
and especially to those who are of the household of faith.

Do you have a friend or family member who could use a
helping hand? God's heart is truly blessed when we are
a blessing to others. What better way to bless someone
than by spending time helping them meet various needs?
Helping others creates a winning situation for everyone
involved. It gives you the satisfaction of knowing that
you've helped someone and it blesses the person in
need as well. Who will you be a blessing to today?

_____

_____

_____

_____

_____

_____

I will let God be God.

PSALM 46:10
Be still, and know that I am God; I will be exalted
among the nations, I will be exalted in the earth!

Have you ever had a young child "assist" with a household
chore or task? With their tiny hands and developing
brains, chances are they haven't quite mastered accuracy,
and that's okay because they are children! It's kind of
the same thing when we attempt to do things that we
should allow God to handle. His ways are higher than
ours, and when we get involved, we make a big mess. Let
God be in control of your life. He makes no mistakes!

I will journal instead of vent on social media.

NUMBERS 11:1 (NIV)
Now the people complained about their hardships in the hearing of the Lord, and when he heard them his anger was aroused. Then fire from the Lord burned among them and consumed some of the outskirts of the camp.

Social media has great uses in this day and age, but using it like your journal or therapist is not one of them! Everything we put on the Internet is public information. Even if your social media profile is locked or private, you have no control over your information being shared without your knowledge. Protect your innermost thoughts and feelings by using your personal diary or journal to vent.

_____

_____

_____

_____

_____

_____

SEPTEMBER 17

I will not judge others based on their appearance.

JOHN 7:24
Stop judging by mere appearances,
but instead judge correctly.

God is concerned with what is in our hearts, not on our bodies. Society places a heavy emphasis on what we wear and how we look. God wants to know how our soul looks. How is your soul adorned? We have been conditioned to judge people by their outward appearance, but God doesn't call us to think that way. Will you commit to seeing people through God's eyes? Stop judging by mere appearances, but instead judge correctly.

_____

_____

_____

_____

_____

_____

_____

I will not project my pain onto others.

2 CORINTHIANS 1:5
For just as we share abundantly in the sufferings of
Christ, so also our comfort abounds through Christ.

Have you ever heard the saying "hurt people hurt
others"? The human psyche is a powerful thing in the
sense that it develops defense mechanisms in order to
protect itself from perceived emotional pain. One of the
ways that this is evident is via projecting that pain onto
someone else. Allow God to heal any pain that you may
feel. Inflicting pain on another person does not solve
anything. In fact, it causes another problem instead.

PSALM 147:3 (KJV)
He healeth the broken in heart, and
bindeth up their wounds.

_____

_____

_____

_____

_____

I will not live in poverty.

PROVERBS 29:13 (ESV)
The poor man and the oppressor meet together;
the Lord gives light to the eyes of both.

God has called us to live in abundance. Poverty is
more than an economic status. It is a mindset. You
could have six figures in your bank account but have
an impoverished mindset. God wants us to live without
lack in our finances and every other aspect of our lives
as well. What areas of your life are impoverished?
Do you believe that God has more for you?

_____

_____

_____

_____

_____

_____

_____

SEPTEMBER 20

I will admit when I am wrong.

PROVERBS 28:13
Whoever conceals his transgressions will not prosper, but
he who confesses and forsakes them will obtain mercy.

Being able to admit when you are wrong takes courage
and humility. Do you have a hard time admitting
when you are wrong? Ask God to soften that part of
your heart that doesn't want to be wrong. It's okay to
make mistakes. None of us are right all of the time.
Don't be afraid of being wrong or admitting to it!

I will not be self-righteous.

PROVERBS 30:12 (NASB)
There is a kind who is pure in his own eyes,
yet is not washed from his filthiness.

God calls us to walk in humility and compassion. Self-righteousness reflects the opposite of these things. A self-righteous person thinks that their flaws are somehow not as bad as another person's. This is simply untrue. We all have shortcomings, and one person's faults are no better or worse than another's. Is there self-righteousness lurking in your heart or your mind? I stand in agreement in prayer with you for God to remove that type of thinking.

I will apologize when necessary.

MATTHEW 5:23-24 (NIV)
Therefore, if you are offering your gift at the altar and
there remember that your brother or sister has something
against you, leave your gift there in front of the altar. First
go and be reconciled to them; then come and offer your gift.

"I'm sorry." Two simple words that can mean so much,
yet be so hard for some to say. Do you have trouble
apologizing? If you answered yes, you certainly are not
alone. With God's help and practice, this can become easier
for you! Don't be afraid to be vulnerable. Apologies set the
stage for healing when there has been brokenness. Is there
someone you need to apologize to? Will you do it today?

I will celebrate the successes of my friends.

ROMANS 12:15
Rejoice with those who rejoice; mourn
with those who mourn.

Success is so much sweeter when you have people to share it with. God is happy when you succeed and he is happy when we celebrate the success of others as well! A congratulatory word can go a long way with the people we care about. Also, you would want some to celebrate your success as well. First demonstrate that with others so that it can happen to you.

SEPTEMBER 24

I will strengthen my prayer life starting today.

PHILIPPIANS 4:6
Do not be anxious about anything, but in
every situation, by prayer and petition, with
thanksgiving, present your requests to God.

How can you strengthen your prayer life? Just like with
most things, the more you do them, the better you become
at them. Prayer is no different. It takes practice. As you
pray more often, you will find yourself becoming more
confident. As you experience God answering your prayers
and communicating with you in your prayer times, you
will find that it becomes second nature to you. God loves
when we come to him in prayer. Have you prayed today?

_____

_____

_____

_____

_____

_____

I will support a local business today.

1 CORINTHIANS 3:9 (WBT)
For we are laborers together with God: ye are
God's husbandry, ye are God's building.

Small businesses are a key factor in boosting our
economy. Also, when we support a small business, we
are supporting a dream. Shop small as often as you
can! What small business will you support today?

_____

_____

_____

_____

_____

_____

_____

_____

_____

I will no longer tolerate what I need to terminate.

HEBREWS 12:1-2 (NIV)
Therefore, since we are surrounded by such a great
cloud of witnesses, let us throw off everything that
hinders and the sin that so easily entangles. And let us
run with perseverance the race marked out for us, fixing
our eyes on Jesus, the pioneer and perfecter of faith.

Are you holding on to things that are dead in your life?
Do you allow things that you should put a stop to? We
all have at some point. The good news is that you are
alive and well, so you still have the opportunity to make
any necessary changes. What have you been tolerating
in your life? Mistreatment? Negative thinking? Financial
irresponsibility? Vices? Make the choice that you will no
longer allow these things to have authority in your life!
God wants to help you to rid your life of things that do not
benefit you or please him. What will you terminate today?

I will seek to please God, not man.

1 Thessalonians 2:4 (ESV)
But just as we have been approved by God to be
entrusted with the gospel, so we speak, not to please
man, but to please God who tests our hearts.

We live in a society that praises seeking man's approval.
For example, the number of "likes" we get on social media.
Falling into the trap of seeking man's approval can be a
dangerous one. We have to condition ourselves to be more
concerned with what God says about us than what man
says. How many "likes" would God give your thoughts,
words, and actions? You will find that God is much more
compassionate than mankind. Aim to please him instead!

I am a peacemaker.

PSALM 34:14 (NIV)
Turn away from evil and do good; seek peace and pursue it.

How can you keep the peace in your surroundings? Have you ever been in a position where you had to act directly in order to de-escalate a situation? If you witness an altercation, will you attempt to help the parties involved come to a peaceful solution? What does peace mean to you?

_____

_____

_____

_____

_____

_____

_____

_____

I will honor the gifts God has given me.

PROVERBS 3:9 (NASB)
Honor the Lord from your wealth and
from the first of all your produce.

What does it mean to honor the gifts that you have been given? First, you must identify your gifts. Secondly, you must use them to bless others. When we utilize our gifts to bless others, we show God that we are appreciative of his blessings. How will you honor your gifts today?

_____

_____

_____

_____

_____

_____

_____

_____

_____

I will show God gratitude by serving His people.

HEBREWS 6:10 (NIV)
God is not unjust; he will not forget your work
and the love you have shown him as you have
helped his people and continue to help them.

How can you be of service to the people of God? Does your
church do any sort of outreach within your community?
Is there a local mentoring program that you can be a part
of? There are many ways that we can serve. When we
embrace a spirit of service, we are truly embodying one of
the sincerest traits of Christ. How will you serve today?

_____

_____

_____

_____

_____

_____

_____

_____

October

I will not miss out on what God has for me.

PSALM 119:105
Your word is a lamp for my feet, a light on my path.

God longs to bless you. He rejoices when you are happy and he sees the very best in you. Don't allow anyone to tell you different, not even yourself.

OCTOBER 2

I will not focus on my problems.

JAMES 4:7 (ESV)
Submit yourselves therefore to God. Resist
the devil, and he will flee from you.

When we are faced with difficult situations, God is
providing us with a chance to increase our faith.
How? By focusing on him instead of the issues
we see. Will you choose to focus on what is going
wrong in your life? Or will you focus on God?

I will keep my vision at the forefront of my mind.

PROVERBS 29:18 (NASB)
Where there is no vision, the people are
unrestrained, but happy is he who keeps the law.

Do you believe in your vision? God gives us goals
and dreams for a reason. When met with adversity,
it is easy to lose sight of our plans. God wants you
to stay focused and stay on track. Don't give up on
reaching for the vision that he has given you.

_____

_____

_____

_____

_____

_____

_____

_____

OCTOBER 4

I am financially sound.

DEUTERONOMY 28:12 (NIV)
The Lord will open the heavens, the storehouse of
his bounty, to send rain on your land in season and
to bless all the work of your hands. You will lend
to many nations but will borrow from none.

To be financially sound means to have security and
stability in your finances. What obstacles are keeping
you from said stability? What actions will you take
to reach a place of financial stability in your life?

_____

_____

_____

_____

_____

_____

_____

_____

I will direct people to the Word of God
when I am given the opportunity.

MATTHEW 24:14 (ESV)
And this gospel of the kingdom will be proclaimed
throughout the whole world as a testimony to
all nations, and then the end will come.

When we witness to others, we glorify God and his power
in our lives. We are so blessed to have God's word as our
reference point. One of the greatest things we can do is
share that word with others. Who will you witness to today?

_____

_____

_____

_____

_____

_____

_____

_____

OCTOBER 6

I will meditate on God's promises.

Psalm 89:34 (NASB)
My covenant I will not violate, nor will
I alter the utterance of my lips.

Do you believe God's promises for your life? Do you trust that they will come to pass? God takes great pleasure in blessing his children, which includes you! I challenge you to accept his promises with authority. Make them personal. Believe that they are for you!

_____

_____

_____

_____

_____

_____

_____

_____

OCTOBER 7

I will not be led astray by false teaching.
–Alexandria L. Barlowe

1 JOHN 4:1 (ESV)
Beloved, do not believe every spirit, but test the
spirits to see whether they are from God, for many
false prophets have gone out into the world.

God calls us to be wise. In practicing wisdom, we can
guard against false teaching. To be able to discern
good teaching from false teaching, you must first
know the character of God. When you understand
what is God's character, it will become easier to spot
someone who is not in alignment with God's word.

_____

_____

_____

_____

_____

_____

_____

I will accept the fact that people will always
disappoint me, but God will never fail me.

DEUTERONOMY 31:8 (NIV)
The Lord himself goes before you and will be
with you; he will never leave you nor forsake you.
Do not be afraid; do not be discouraged.

It's not fun to feel as if someone has let you down. This
feeling can cause us to lose trust and stop believing
in people. When we realize that we are flawed human
beings, we understand that people may fail, but our God
is incapable of failure. Take comfort in knowing that
regardless of the heart of man, God is always on time.

_____

_____

_____

_____

_____

_____

_____

OCTOBER 9

I will walk in love and light.

JOHN 8:12

When Jesus spoke again to the people, he said, "I am
the light of the world. Whoever follows me will never
walk in darkness, but will have the light of life."

God's greatest command to us is to love. God is all things
love and all things light. There is no darkness in the
character of God. He may allow us to experience periods
of darkness, but he in himself is only light. To walk in these
aspects of God is to be truly like him. What does this mean
to you? How will you practice walking in love and light?

_____

_____

_____

_____

_____

_____

_____

OCTOBER 10

I will exude confidence in my abilities.

PROVERBS 3:26 (ESV)
For the Lord will be your confidence and
will keep your foot from being caught.

God made you with innate abilities. He also blessed you
with the aptitude to be able to learn new things. In this,
always be confident. God loves when we feel secure in the
things that we are able to do. He considers your abilities
a celebration of the fact that you were fearfully and
wonderfully made. Will you walk in confidence today?

OCTOBER 11

I will be appreciative of people who have
given me their time and resources.

PSALM 106:1 (NIV)
Praise the Lord. Give thanks to the Lord, for
he is good; his love endures forever.

You may have heard the expression, "time is money."
This is true and it is important to understand how
valuable someone's time is. If you have been fortunate
enough to receive the blessing of someone's time and
resources, be sure to be thankful. Don't take it for granted
that someone has blessed you. Will you reach out to
someone who has given you some of their time today?

_____

_____

_____

_____

_____

_____

_____

I will be thankful for the little things.

PSALM 95:2-3

Let us come before him with thanksgiving and
extol him with music and song. For the Lord is
the great God, the great King above all gods.

What little things make you happy? Maybe something as
simple as the sunlight peeking through your window in
the morning? Or the sound of your children's feet running
up and down the stairs? Perhaps it is a phone call from a
loved one, just to say hello. Whatever the little things are in
your life, be sure to take a moment just to say thank you.

OCTOBER 13

I will be obedient to God's word.

1 SAMUEL 15:22
But Samuel replied: Does the Lord delight in
burnt offerings and sacrifices as much as in
obeying the Lord? To obey is better than sacrifice,
and to heed is better than the fat of rams.

Have you ever tried to put together a piece of furniture
or appliance without reading the instructions first?
Attempting to live a Christian lifestyle without reading
God's word is very similar. God's word is our instruction
manual. Without reading it, we will undoubtedly
make more than a few mistakes. Read and take heed
to his word. It is the best way to know his heart.

_____

_____

_____

_____

_____

_____

_____

I will not confuse God's word with man's opinion.
–Alexandria L. Barlowe

HEBREWS 4:12
For the word of God is alive and active. Sharper
than any double-edged sword, it penetrates even
to dividing soul and spirit, joints and marrow; it
judges the thoughts and attitudes of the heart.

What God says is more important than anything else in
our lives. He reigns supreme and he has given us his word
to guide us in our daily lives. We must know that pastors,
preachers, evangelists, prophets, etc., are men and women
of God who are called to preach God's word, not their
own word. When we listen to them, we should follow
after them as they follow God. Fellowship and church
membership is a blessing from God, but we must be careful
not to confuse the woman or man with the message.

_____

_____

_____

_____

_____

I will live in a way that honors God.

ROMANS 12:1

Therefore, I urge you, brothers and sisters, in view of God's mercy, to offer your bodies as a living sacrifice, holy and pleasing to God—this is your true and proper worship.

Would someone know or believe that you were a Christian if you never told them? Would they be able to tell by how you speak? By how you act? God calls us to represent him in everything that we do. His light should be so visible in your character that people know you are a believer before you even mention it. I challenge you to tackle the answers to these questions head on. If the answer is no to any of them, I am standing in prayer with you right now. You are precious in God's eyes, and he wants you to be a beacon of hope to everyone you meet. Will you let him shine through you today?

I will be tolerant of people who are different than me.

ROMANS 14:2-4

One person's faith allows them to eat anything, but another, whose faith is weak, eats only vegetables. The one who eats everything must not treat with contempt the one who does not, and the one who does not eat everything must not judge the one who does, for God has accepted them. Who are you to judge someone else's servant? To their own master, servants stand or fall. And they will stand, for the Lord is able to make them stand.

Wouldn't the world be a boring place if we were all the same? Diversity is one of the gifts God has given us. He wants us to accept and embrace the differences we have with our peers. Always be careful to treat others with kindness regardless of their religious beliefs, political views, sexual orientation, and socioeconomic status. We are all part of the human race regardless of our various differences. That is enough commonality to merit common decency.

OCTOBER 17

I will be wise with my time on social media.

EPHESIANS 5:15-17 (ESV)
Look carefully then how you walk, not as unwise but
as wise, making the best use of the time, because
the days are evil. Therefore do not be foolish,
but understand what the will of the Lord is.

Social media is one of the biggest popular culture
phenomena of our time. It has influenced political
campaigns, turned virtually unknown people into
household names, and given us a closer look into the lives
of our favorite public figures. It is both a blessing and a
curse. It can be a very effective marketing tool for your
business and brand, but it can also be a big distraction,
if you let it. Be sure that you don't use social media to
compare yourself to others, engage in debates that can
turn ugly, or keep in touch with exes. These are situations
that can spiral out of control quickly if we are not careful.

I will pray for those in leadership.

ROMANS 13:1
Let every person be subject to the governing authorities. For there is no authority except from God, and those that exist have been instituted by God.

People in positions of leadership are often the first to be criticized. In this day and age of social media, this is perhaps truer than it has ever been. I challenge you to pray for our leaders when you catch yourself being critical of them. Leaders on every level face immense pressure and are forced to make difficult decisions. I stand in prayer with you for every leader in our country.

_____

_____

_____

_____

_____

_____

_____

OCTOBER 19

I am enough.

ISAIAH 43:4 (NLT)
Others were given in exchange for you. I traded
their lives for yours because you are precious
to me. You are honored, and I love you.

One of the main things that inspired me to write this
book was the need for people to increase their self-
esteem, self-value, and confidence. I want you to know
what I already know with great certainty: you are loved.
You are special and a valuable asset to God's kingdom.
I do not care what people have told you prior to this
moment, because if it was anything other than that you
are loved and enough, it was not the truth. I wish you
could see you the way God sees you. You are the apple
of his eye and worth the sacrifice of his only begotten
son. You mean so much to God. Please dwell on
nothing but this throughout the day. You are enough!

OCTOBER 20

I will do something special for my spouse today.

EPHESIANS 4:2 (NIV)
Be completely humble and gentle; be patient,
bearing with one another in love.

There are few things sweeter than a thoughtful act from
your spouse. It could be something small like surprising
them with their favorite meal or buying them a thoughtful
gift that commemorates your first date. It's the thought
that counts here, so go as big or as small as you like. The
element of surprise is a powerful tool that keeps your
relationship fresh and exciting. God is pleased when we
are in a healthy place with our spouses. Enjoy the look on
your love's face when met with your special thought or gift.

OCTOBER 21

I will have an attitude of gratitude.

COLOSSIANS 4:2 (NIV)
Devote yourselves to prayer, being watchful and thankful.

What does gratitude mean to you? What things are you
thankful for? When we focus our energy on the things that
we are grateful for, our world seems to get a little sweeter.
I challenge you to take five minutes today to either write or
speak out loud five things that you are grateful for. Make
an effort to meditate on those things throughout your day.

_____

_____

_____

_____

_____

_____

_____

_____

I will create a budget and stick to it!

1 CORINTHIANS 4:2 (ESV)
Moreover, it is required of stewards
that they be found faithful.

Budgeting is all about discipline. It may seem difficult if it is not something you are used to, but it is simply planning and allocating cash flow and managing accordingly. Start by making a list of your expenses. Create room in your budget for things that you like, e.g., date nights, Starbucks, or salon and spa services. You will notice that budgeting gets easier the more you do it. You will also feel more at peace knowing exactly where your money is going every month.

OCTOBER 23

I will give up vices that are bad for my
physical or emotional health.

1 PETER 5:8
Be sober-minded; be watchful. Your adversary
the devil prowls around like a roaring
lion, seeking someone to devour.

In many cases, we engage in vices as a way of escape.
God wants to be your way of escape. He does not
want you to be entangled in the bondage of addiction.
God loves you. He longs for relationship with you.
In his loving arms, he has every route of escape
that you need. Will you embrace him today?

I will praise a colleague for his or her
work on a recent project.

ROMANS 15:2 (NIV)
Each of us should please our neighbors
for their good, to build them up.

Having your great performance recognized is an excellent
confidence booster. Work assignments often require a lot
of time and effort, and it is a blessing to have that effort
recognized. When we give kudos to our colleagues, we
invite them to do the same when we perform well.

I will find new ways to excel in my career.

2 CORINTHIANS 8:7 (NET)
But as you excel in everything—in faith, in
speech, in knowledge, and in all eagerness and
in the love from us that is in you—make sure
that you excel in this act of kindness too.

Employment is a blessing, and we give God glory
when we excel in our careers. Are there new skills
you could learn or new certifications that would help
you advance? Are there projects that you can be a
part of that would expose you to new aspects of your
job? Ask God to give you ideas and innovations on
how you can take your career to the next level!

I will mentor a young person who reminds me of myself.

PSALM 145:4 (ESV)
One generation shall commend your works to
another, and shall declare your mighty acts.

Do you know a young person who could benefit from
your wisdom and experiences? Maybe they are going
through a situation that you have been through. God
calls us to help others in any way that we can. Youth
are the future leaders of our world, and we owe it to
them to share the knowledge we have gained. Whether
it be helping them apply to college or simply listening
to what their favorite after-school activities are, I
encourage you to find a young person to mentor!

OCTOBER 27

I will remember that I am loved.

ROMANS 5:8 (NIV)
But God demonstrates his own love for us in this:
While we were still sinners, Christ died for us.

There are simply not enough words in the human
vocabulary to explain just how much God loves
you. He hurts when we hurt and he is truly happy
when we are happy. Please, if you don't remember
anything else today, remember that you are loved!

_____

_____

_____

_____

_____

_____

_____

I will stop being too hard on myself.

EPHESIANS 2:4
But because of his great love for us,
God, who is rich in mercy.

Have you heard the expression "you are your own worst
critic"? Are you constantly beating yourself up or feeling
like you'll never get "it" right? Anything that is worth having
is going to have its challenges. God wants you to be patient
with yourself. He acknowledges your efforts and he does
not expect perfection. As long as you are giving it your all,
give yourself a break if you miss your target. Just as the old
adage says, "if at first you don't succeed, try, try again."

_____

_____

_____

_____

_____

_____

_____

OCTOBER 29

I will not become stagnant or complacent in my situation.

MATTHEW 7:20 (NHEB)
Therefore, by their fruits you will know them.

We serve a God of progression and forward
movement. He calls us to be fruitful, which means
to be productive. Are you in a phase of complacency
in your life? God wants to propel you forward to
action. I encourage you to let his word energize and
ignite your life and watch amazing things happen!

_____

_____

_____

_____

_____

_____

_____

_____

_____

I will stop comparing my life to the lives of celebrities.

2 CORINTHIANS 10:12 (NIV)
We do not dare to classify or compare ourselves
with some who commend themselves. When they
measure themselves by themselves and compare
themselves with themselves, they are not wise.

The images we see in media are made to entertain us.
They are not real! Yes, celebrities are real people, but their
careers place them in situations that are not realistic for
the average person. It is easy to see them on television
and in magazines and to feel envy for their lifestyle,
but remember, it's not real! Celebrities have a staff of
people who are paid to make sure they look perfect at all
times. It is unfair to compare yourself to said standard.
You are absolutely wonderful just the way you are.

_____

_____

_____

_____

_____

I will sing praise and worship songs
on my way to work today.

PSALM 33:1-3 (NASB)

Sing for joy in the Lord, O you righteous ones; praise is becoming to the upright. Give thanks to the lord with the lyre; sing praises to Him with a harp of ten strings. Sing to Him a new song; play skillfully with a shout of joy.

The power of praise and worship is beyond explanation. When you praise and worship God, there is a shift in the atmosphere. When we usher God's presence into our lives, he moves! He meets us where we are and ministers to our needs. I dare you to start your day with praise and see how God's presence reflects throughout the rest of your day.

_____

_____

_____

_____

_____

_____

November

I will talk to a counselor about unresolved emotional issues.

1 Peter 5:10 (ESV)
And after you have suffered a little while, the God of all grace, who has called you to his eternal glory in Christ, will himself restore, confirm, strengthen and establish you.

There is often a negative stigma attached to seeking help from mental health professionals. I am here to tell you that God has blessed us with earthly help that can truly bless us. There is nothing wrong with seeking help from a therapist or counselor. I encourage you to get the help that you need. I rebuke any spirit that tries to tell you otherwise. Everyone responds differently to the things that we experience in life. God knows that and wants you to reach out for help to heal issues that have gone unresolved in your life. Will you make the call to get help today?

_____

_____

_____

_____

_____

I will allow God to release me from
the bondage of my past hurts.

2 CORINTHIANS 3:17 (NIV)
Now the Lord is the Spirit, and where the
Spirit of the Lord is, there is freedom.

Aren't we blessed to serve a God who calls us to be
free? He loves you so very much and he did not design
the things in your past to keep you in chains. You can
be free. You can reclaim your life. Your past does not
define you. You are a wonderful creature in Christ, and
it is time for you to stand up and walk in your freedom!

_____

_____

_____

_____

_____

_____

_____

I will stop making excuses for bad behavior.

2 CORINTHIANS 5:10 (ESV)
For we must all appear before the judgment seat of
Christ, so that each one may receive what is due for
what he has done in the body, whether good or evil.

Have you found yourself in a cycle of making bad decisions?
We have all been there. Don't be down on yourself.
Instead, take complete responsibility for your choices and
commit to making a change. God loves you so much. He
wants to see you succeed. Start by repenting. Tell God
that you want to change. You can change. You are better
than the bad choices that you have been making. You are
a child of the King. You are the seed of righteousness. It
is within you to do right! I believe in you and I trust God
in agreement with you for positive change in your life!

I will align myself with like-minded people.

PHILIPPIANS 2:2 (NIV)
Then make my joy complete by being like-minded, having the same love, being one in spirit and of one mind.

Have you ever found yourself within a group of friends that you had nothing in common with? With respect to our friends and people we choose to associate closely with, we should seek others who share our same values and love for Christ. Is your current group of friends in alignment with the principles that govern your life?

_____

_____

_____

_____

_____

_____

_____

I will work well with others, even if our personalities clash.

EPHESIANS 4:16 (ESV)
From whom the whole body, joined and held
together by every joint with which it is equipped,
when each part is working properly, makes the
body grow so that it builds itself up in love.

We all have that one person (or few people) who we
do not vibe well with. God made mankind with many
diverse personality types, and some of those personalities
are bound to clash from time to time. It is not easy
to work with someone you don't get along with, but
God calls us to be peaceable, even in undesirable
situations. If you are working with someone whose
personality clashes with yours, I challenge you to pray
for that person. Pray that God helps you to work on
one accord with them in spite of your differences.

I will speak up for myself.

EPHESIANS 6:10 (NIV)
Finally, be strong in the Lord and in his mighty power.

Have you ever wanted to speak up about something but you were too afraid? God wants us to be strong in him. Don't be afraid to speak the truth or speak up for yourself. God commands us to be of good courage several times throughout his word. He wants you to speak the truth and speak up for yourself, even if your voice shakes!

_____

_____

_____

_____

_____

_____

_____

_____

_____

I will not ignore physical signs that could
potentially indicate a health problem.

JEREMIAH 33:6
Nevertheless, I will bring health and healing
to it; I will heal my people and will let them
enjoy abundant peace and security.

God created our bodies with systems to warn us
when something is not right. That nagging pain you've
been experiencing for several months could be one of
those warning signs. Don't put off a visit to the doctor
because you are afraid. God is the chief physician
and he wants our bodies to function well, as they
are supposed to. He has provided us with medical
experts here on Earth to ensure that we are well.
Will you make that doctor's appointment today?

NOVEMBER 8

I will not walk in depression.

PSALM 42:11
Why, my soul, are you downcast? Why so
disturbed within me? Put your hope in God, for I
will yet praise him, my Savior and my God.

Depression is a very real issue that can leave its sufferers
feeling completely hopeless. There is hope in our Lord
and Savior. The holiday season can be the hardest for
those who battle depression. If you are having a difficult
time, please do not hide it or pretend that everything is
okay. God wants to heal you. You do not have to suffer in
silence. If you know someone who is battling depression,
pray with them and encourage them to seek help as well.

NOVEMBER 9

I will stop existing and start living.

JAMES 4:14 (ESV)
Yet you do not know what tomorrow will bring.
What is your life? For you are a mist that
appears for a little time and then vanishes.

Do you feel like you are going through the motions
on a daily basis? God wants us to live a vibrant and
exciting life! He wants our lives to be enriched by
meaningful experiences. What do you feel is holding
you back from living a life that you love? I pray that
you find out what makes you feel as if you are living
and not just existing, and pursue it vigorously!

NOVEMBER 10

I will be aware of the enemy's devices.

2 Corinthians 2:11 (NIV)
In order that Satan might not outwit us. For
we are not unaware of his schemes.

When we know and understand how the enemy
works, we aren't surprised when he tests us or sends
temptation our way. The enemy holds no punches and
never fights fair; but God! You serve the true and living
God, and he is on your side. You have nothing to fear!

_____

_____

_____

_____

_____

_____

_____

_____

_____

I believe that God will lift me when I am down.

PSALM 145:14
The Lord upholds all who fall and lifts
up all who are bowed down.

God is our biggest cheerleader! He is always rooting
for us and takes pleasure in turning sorrow into joy.
Are you in the midst of a sad season right now? Be
encouraged. God loves you and he hears your cries. He
will lift your head and put a smile back on your face.

I will not get in God's way.

ISAIAH 55:9 (ESV)
For as the heavens are higher than the earth,
so are my ways higher than your ways and
my thoughts than your thoughts.

Do you trust that God has your situation under control? He does. Let him have his way in your life. If he has closed a door, don't try to reopen it. If he has delivered you from something or someone, don't return to that place of bondage. Let God do his work and fall in line with his plan for your life.

_____

_____

_____

_____

_____

_____

_____

I will become active in my church community.

PSALM 55:14 (NASB)
We who had sweet fellowship together walked
in the house of God in the throng.

Fellowship with our brothers and sisters in Christ is one
of the many gifts God has blessed us with. He is blessed
by our service to our respective houses of worship. How
can you get involved at your church home today?

_____

_____

_____

_____

_____

_____

_____

_____

I will not get advice from someone who has not
experienced what I am going through.

PROVERBS 11:14 (ESV)
Where there is no guidance, a people falls, but in
an abundance of counselors there is safety.

Good counsel is very valuable. It can be the difference
between a good outcome and a bad outcome in your life.
If you go to someone for advice, be sure that they are
anointed with God's wisdom and that they have experience
in the subject at hand. Are you receiving good advice?

_____

_____

_____

_____

_____

_____

_____

_____

I will not believe lies.

GALATIANS 6:7 (NIV)
Do not be deceived: God cannot be mocked.
A man reaps what he sows.

God is an honest God. He does not operate where there is untruth. He did not call and choose us to be deceived. Pray that God reveals the untruths in your life. Ask him to give you the wisdom and discernment to know the difference between lies and truth. Trust and believe in him. He will make these things known to you.

_____

_____

_____

_____

_____

_____

_____

_____

I will not allow people to manipulate me.

MATTHEW 24:4
And Jesus answered them, "See that
no one leads you astray."

Manipulation is rooted in deception. Often, people who are manipulative have a strong need for control; therefore, they deceive others in order to gain that control. God is not a manipulative God. He is all things true and good. Is there someone in your life who is constantly trying to manipulate you? I stand in agreement with you right now that God remove that force in your life. I consider it done in Jesus' name.

_____

_____

_____

_____

_____

_____

_____

I will not manipulate others.

JAMES 2:12 (ESV)
So speak and so act as those who are to
be judged under the law of liberty.

Just as we should not allow ourselves to be manipulated,
we should not in any way manipulate others. Do you
have issues with trying to bend people's will to coincide
with yours? God wants you to surrender to him and
know that only he is in control. Will you abandon
all manipulative thoughts and behaviors today?

NOVEMBER 18

I will not allow my circumstances to derail my faith.

GALATIANS 6:9 (NIV)
Let us not become weary in doing good, for at the proper
time we will reap a harvest if we do not give up.

God sits on the throne and sees all. He knows that
your situation is trying right now. Stand strong in him!
Don't let your faith be shaken! God is going to move in
a great way in your life. I believe it. Do you believe it?

NOVEMBER 19

I will place my trust in God.

ISAIAH 40:31 (NLT)
But those whose trust is in the Lord will find new strength.
They will soar high on wings like eagles. They will run
and not grow weary. They will walk and not faint.

The song "What a Friend We Have in Jesus" says, "what
a privilege to carry everything to God in prayer." Do you
trust that God has your best interest at heart? When
you begin to really trust God, you will experience true
peace. He wants that for you! Will you trust him?

NOVEMBER 20

I will pray for wisdom.

PROVERBS 4:7 (NIV)
The beginning of wisdom is this: Get wisdom.
Though it cost all you have, get understanding.

God calls us to be wise and discerning. Operating
in wisdom is being able to see the surface as well
as what is beneath the surface of something. God
wants to seek wisdom more than we seek material
things. I stand with you in prayer today for wisdom.

_____

_____

_____

_____

_____

_____

_____

_____

_____

I will stop thinking that I don't need God.

1 PETER 5:6 (ESV)
Humble yourselves, therefore, under the mighty hand
of God so that at the proper time he may exalt you.

We all need God. God is very good at showing us that we
need him. He created us to need him. Are you walking
through life under the misconception that you do not need
him? That you are just fine on your own? My beloved friend,
you do need him. More importantly, he is here for you!
Will you accept him and seek his presence in your life?

I am a strategic thinker.

PROVERBS 16:9 (NIV)
In their hearts humans plan their course,
but the Lord establishes their steps.

God loves things that are done decently and in order.
When we are strategic in our thinking, we honor him.
Having a plan and approaching situations strategically
is one small way that we can be Christ like. How
will you be strategic in your thinking today?

_____

_____

_____

_____

_____

_____

_____

_____

_____

I will be thankful all year round.

PSALM 9:1
I will give thanks to you, Lord, with all my heart;
I will tell of all your wonderful deeds.

We are so richly blessed by God. We have so many things
to be thankful for. Find a few moments to write a list of
all the things that you are thankful for today. You might be
surprised to see how long that list is. I am thankful for you!

_____

_____

_____

_____

_____

_____

_____

_____

I will be known for my kindness and love toward others.

GENESIS 24:14

May it be that when I say to a young woman, "Please let down your jar that I may have a drink," and she says, "Drink, and I'll water your camels too"—let her be the one you have chosen for your servant Isaac. By this I will know that you have shown kindness to my master.

This chapter in Genesis is about Isaac and Rebekah. In this particular passage of scripture, Rebekah is recognized by her kindness. We should also seek to be known for our kindness. To be truly Christ like in our daily living, we must exude kindness and the love of God. How will you show someone kindness and love today?

_____

_____

_____

_____

_____

_____

I will be honest about my feelings.

ECCLESIASTES 3:4 (NASB)
A time to weep and a time to laugh; A time
to mourn and a time to dance.

Have you ever replied "fine" when asked how you
were doing, in spite of how you really felt? Be sure
to acknowledge your true feelings to yourself. If you
are not fine, ask yourself why. When we are honest
with ourselves about our innermost feelings, we
can look to God to help us in the areas we need him
the most. Honestly, how are you feeling today?

_____

NOVEMBER 26

I will take the necessary steps to establish
my business the right way.

1 CORINTHIANS 14:40 (ESV)
But all things should be done decently and in order.

When you decide that you want to go into business,
there are steps and procedures that you need to follow.
For example, registering your business name, ensuring
that you have a tax ID number, opening a business
bank account, etc. God wants us to be in order in
everything that we do. What steps will you take to ensure
that your business is established properly today?

_____

_____

_____

_____

_____

_____

_____

I will be myself, authentically and unapologetically.

PHILIPPIANS 1:27
Only let your manner of life be worthy of the
gospel of Christ, so that whether I come and
see you or am absent, I may hear of you that you
are standing firm in one spirit, with one mind
striving side by side for the faith of the gospel.

God created all that is you. Your eyes, your hair, your
nose, your personality traits, your voice, and your spirit.
He loves you in every way and wants you to love who
you are as well. Be who you are and don't apologize for
it! Always be authentic in everything that you do and
know that when God made you, he was pleased!

NOVEMBER 28

I will treat people in a way that glorifies God.

LUKE 6:31
And as you wish that others would do to you, do so to them.

As Christians, we are God's earthly representatives. Just as
representatives for big corporations must be in line with
their company's mission and vision, we must be in line with
the missions and vision of Christ. Would people around you
know that you are a believer based on how you treat them?
Does your treatment of others glorify God? If not, I stand
with you in prayer today. God can change your heart and
help you to treat others with the same love that he would.

NOVEMBER 29

I will allow myself to grieve the loss of a loved one.
–Alexandria L. Barlowe

PSALM 116:15 (NIV)
Precious in the sight of the Lord is the
death of his faithful servants.

It is never easy to cope with the death of someone we love. Regardless of the circumstances surrounding their death, we are left with a gaping hole once their earthly presence is no more. While it doesn't get easier to live without that loved one, we are fortunate to have a God to turn to when we are hurting. We must allow ourselves to feel that pain. It doesn't make you weak and it doesn't do you any harm to remember the times you had with your late family member or friend. Those memories of them are how we keep their legacies alive.

NOVEMBER 30

I will show compassion to my enemies.

PROVERBS 24:17 (ESV)
Do not rejoice when your enemy falls, and let
not your heart be glad when he stumbles.

Have you ever found yourself saying "that's what he/
she gets"? It is so natural to feel glad when someone
who has wronged us is hurting, but this is not
what God wants of us. It is challenging, but pray
that God give you an understanding heart. Always
be compassionate when an enemy is in pain.

December

I will let God use me.

JOHN 12:26

If anyone serves me, he must follow me; and
where I am, there will my servant be also. If
anyone serves me, the Father will honor him.

God takes great pride in working through his children.
When we allow God to use us, we are helping to further
his plan and purpose for our lives and the lives of those
we help. How will you allow God to use you today?

DECEMBER 2

I will use what I have been through to
help someone else break through.

GALATIANS 5:13
For you were called to freedom, brothers. Only
do not use your freedom as an opportunity for
the flesh, but through love serve one another.

God loves to use experiences to teach us lessons.
He gets all the glory and honor when we help
people with the wisdom we gain from those
experiences. He strategically places people in your
life who can benefit from your testimony. Will you
play a part in someone's breakthrough today?

I believe that one touch of God's favor is all I need.

MATTHEW 9:20-22

Just then a woman who had been subject to bleeding
for twelve years came up behind him and touched the
edge of his cloak. She said to herself, "If I only touch
his cloak, I will be healed. Jesus turned and saw her.
"Take heart, daughter," he said, "your faith has healed
you." And the woman was healed at that moment.

Just like the woman with the issue of blood who was healed
with one touch, you too just need one touch. That one touch
is mighty and can make great changes in your life. Do you
believe? Will you seek God's face for that one touch today?

_____

_____

_____

_____

_____

_____

_____

I will listen and speak as the Holy Spirit speaks to me.

ACTS 2:4
And they were all filled with the Holy Spirit and began to speak in other tongues as the Spirit gave them utterance.

There is power in heavenly language. When we listen to and are filled with his spirit, amazing things can happen. Have you been denying that spirit? Don't be afraid because you think it sounds strange. The Holy Spirit wants to speak to you and through you. Will you let him?

I will not remain in bondage.

LEVITICUS 26:13 (NASB)

I am the Lord your God, who brought you out of the
land of Egypt so that you would not be their slaves, and
I broke the bars of your yoke and made you walk erect.

Aren't we so blessed to serve a God who wants us to
walk in freedom? God has not called us to be enslaved
to anything or anyone. Are you struggling in a place
of bondage in your life? I stand and agree with you
right now that you be released from whatever has a
hold on you. Walk in your freedom! It is yours!

I will give someone who has wronged
me the benefit of the doubt.

MATTHEW 7:3 (NIV)
Why do you look at the speck of sawdust in your brother's
eye and pay no attention to the plank in your own eye?

You may ask, why should I give them the benefit of the
doubt? They hurt me! We have all been guilty of hurting
someone before, whether it was intentional or not.
We must learn to look at people through God's eyes
and also realize that none of us are without fault.

_____

_____

_____

_____

_____

_____

_____

_____

DECEMBER 7

I will walk in honesty and integrity.

PROVERBS 12:22
The Lord detests lying lips, but he delights
in people who are trustworthy.

Being honest and a person of integrity is always the most
difficult when we are under pressure. Under pressure to
hit a certain sales goal at work, under financial pressure
to pay a certain bill, under pressure of potentially getting
in trouble for admitting to something, etc. It is in these
times that the core essence of our values are tested. It's
like when you are faced with making a decision and you
think, what would Jesus do? He would be honest and
operate within integrity no matter what! Will you follow
his lead when faced with a tough decision today?

_____

_____

_____

_____

_____

_____

I will not discipline my children when I am angry.

COLOSSIANS 3:21 (ESV)
Fathers, do not provoke your children,
lest they become discouraged.

As much as we love our children, they have the ability
to get under our skin quicker than anyone else! Their
young minds are always going a mile a minute, and they
have more energy than they know what to do with. They
are going to misbehave sometimes. It is our duty as
their parents to discipline them with the sole purpose of
instructing and redirecting, not to blow off steam. In the
heat of the moment, it can be easy to snap and act in anger.
I challenge you to take a deep breath and think before you
discipline your child. Ask yourself, "am I about to act in
anger?" If the answer is yes, let yourself cool down before
you address your child. Children are one of the greatest
gifts we could ever be blessed with. We owe it to them
and to God to discipline them correctly and in love.

_____

_____

_____

_____

I will not settle for a discount relationship
because I am lonely.

HEBREWS 11:6
And without faith it is impossible to please him, for
whoever would draw near to God must believe that
he exists and that he rewards those who seek him.

Let's take a closer look at what it means to settle. In this
context, it means to accept an option that is conveniently
available to you regardless of its value. Accepting the
convenient option is telling God that we don't have faith
that he will give us what we want. When you have full
confidence that God is going to bring you the desire of
your heart, you don't accept anything less. We have to think
like this when it comes to our personal relationships.

_____

_____

_____

_____

_____

_____

I will not operate in carnality.

1 JOHN 2:16 (NASB)
For all that is in the world, the lust of the flesh and
the lust of the eyes and the boastful pride of life,
is not from the Father, but is from the world.

God calls us to operate in him on matters of the spirit.
When we do so, we are able to receive direction from him.
Operating in our flesh diminishes his presence in our lives.
Allow God to take over and strive to be on one accord
with him. How will you strengthen your spirit today?

_____

_____

_____

_____

_____

_____

_____

_____

I love God for who he is, not because
of what he can do for me.

LUKE 10:27 (ESV)
And he answered, "You shall love the Lord your
God with all your heart and with all your soul
and with all your strength and with all your
mind, and your neighbor as yourself."

God longs to be in relationship with you. He loves you
unconditionally. He knows your innermost battles, yet
he still loves you. He deserves our unconditional love in
return because he is a good and faithful God; not just
because he is able to supply all of our wants and needs.

___

___

___

___

___

___

___

DECEMBER 12

I will not base my happiness on the
actions of another person.

1 CORINTHIANS 14:20
Brothers, do not be children in your thinking. Be
infants in evil, but in your thinking be mature.

When we allow someone else's actions to dictate how
we feel, we are setting ourselves up to be disappointed.
The truth is that happiness is a choice. God wants you
to be happy. Will you choose to be happy today?

DECEMBER 13

I will not be a toxic friend.

PROVERBS 12:26 (NASB)
The righteous is a guide to his neighbor, but
the way of the wicked leads them astray.

God calls us to be a blessing to our friends. He wants
to use us to show them his love and faithfulness. Toxic
friends are a hindrance. Are you a toxic friend? If so,
God can help you change. I am praying for and with
you that God helps you to abandon any behaviors
that can be hurtful to others. God loves you!

_____

_____

_____

_____

_____

_____

_____

_____

DECEMBER 14

I will seek out an expert in my field and
learn all that I can from them.

PSALM 71:18 (ESV)
So even to old age and gray hairs, O God, do not
forsake me, until I proclaim your might to another
generation, your power to all those who come.

We have much to gain from the wisdom of others who
are successful in our field. If you are fortunate enough to
have access to someone who is knowledgeable about the
industry that you are in, take advantage of their expertise.

I will give my goals a realistic deadline.

PSALM 37:4 (NIV)
Take delight in the Lord, and he will give
you the desires of your heart.

God loves when we set goals and work to achieve them!
He longs to give you the desire of your heart. He also
uses the process that we go through to achieve our
goals to teach us things about Him, about ourselves,
and about others. I pray that you understand the
lessons God is showing you in your time of goal-setting!
How will you glorify him with your goal-setting?

_____

_____

_____

_____

_____

_____

_____

DECEMBER 16

I will invite a friend in need to spend
time with me and my family.

PROVERBS 11:25 (NIV)
A generous person will prosper; whoever
refreshes others will be refreshed.

God loves when we are kind to others. He is glorified
when we are there for others. Is there someone in your
life who doesn't have family in town? Invite them over for
a fun night of dinner and board games. It may seem like
a small gesture, but you don't know how much this will
bless them. Your invitation could be an answered prayer.

_____

_____

_____

_____

_____

_____

_____

I will visit an elderly relative who I haven't seen in a while.

LEVITICUS 19:32 (NASB)
You shall rise up before the grayheaded and honor the aged, and you shall revere your God; I am the Lord.

Our elders have a great amount of wisdom that we can benefit from. They have seen things and experienced world events that we could not even begin to understand. Spend time with an older relative this week. Offer to cook them a meal or help with a few chores. Also, be sure to ask them about some of their most memorable moments.

_____

_____

_____

_____

_____

_____

_____

_____

I will ask my spouse "what can I do or say
to make your day better today?"

EPHESIANS 5:25 (NIV)
Husbands, love your wives, just as Christ loved
the church and gave himself up for her.

This scripture may be worded specifically for husbands,
but it can also be interpreted to apply to marital love as a
whole. Practice finding ways to make your spouse smile
each and every day. What will you do for your spouse today?

_____

_____

_____

_____

_____

_____

_____

_____

_____

_____

I will find the beauty in everything.

2 CORINTHIANS 4:16
Therefore we do not lose heart. Though
outwardly we are wasting away, yet inwardly
we are being renewed day by day.

It is easy to find the beauty in our lives when things are
going well. What about when everything in your world
seems to be falling apart at the seams? In those times,
God does his greatest work. Realize that your time
of trouble is teaching you a powerful lesson. There is
beauty in learning and growing from your trials and
tribulations. What situation will you find beauty in today?

_____

_____

_____

_____

_____

_____

_____

I will not go into debt to buy Christmas gifts.

ISAIAH 7:14
Therefore the Lord himself will give you a
sign: The virgin will conceive and give birth
to a son, and will call him Immanuel.

For many, this is the most wonderful time of the
year. It is important to remember the reason for this
joyous time! Christmas gifts are wonderful, but don't
feel so pressured to buy material things that you
put yourself into financial hardship. There are many
ways to give and be a blessing in this season.

_____

_____

_____

_____

_____

_____

_____

I will be in prayer for those who are reminded
of tragedy during this season.

PSALM 34:18 (ESV)
The Lord is near to the brokenhearted
and saves the crushed in spirit.

The holidays can be very difficult for those who are grieving
the loss of a loved one, experiencing financial loss, going
through a divorce, etc. Take time to think of those who are
not feeling merry or bright this season. Reach out to them
and keep them uplifted in prayer. If you are struggling with
feelings of sadness this season, I pray that the healing
balm of God's love meets you where you are right now.
God is with you, and this season will not last forever.

_____

_____

_____

_____

_____

_____

DECEMBER 22

I will value people, memories, and
experiences over material things.

1 Timothy 6:7-8 (NIV)
For we brought nothing into the world, and we
can take nothing out of it. But if we have food
and clothing, we will be content with that.

The most valuable parts of our lives cannot be
bought. Be sure that your focus is on your family
this season! Love and cherish them. Spend as
much time as you can with them. God gave us the
greatest gift when he blessed us with family.

_____

_____

_____

_____

_____

_____

_____

I will keep family traditions no matter how small.

2 THESSALONIANS 2:15 (ESV)
So then, brothers, stand firm and hold to the
traditions that you were taught by us, either
by our spoken word or by our letter.

Making memories with our loved ones helps
deepen our bonds as well as keep traditions alive
throughout generations. What are some of your
family's favorite traditions? What new traditions
would you like to start with your loved ones?

_____

_____

_____

_____

_____

_____

_____

I will praise and worship with my family.

1 CHRONICLES 16:34 (NIV)
Give thanks to the Lord, for he is good;
his love endures forever.

God loves nothing more than when we uplift his name with the people we love the most. Spend time in the Lord with your loved ones. Whether at church on Sunday morning or in your living room, God is pleased when we worship with our families.

DECEMBER 25

I will celebrate the birth of Jesus Christ.

ISAIAH 9:6-7 (NKJV)
For unto us a Child is born, Unto us a Son is given;
And the government will be on His shoulder. And
his name will be called Wonderful, Counselor,
Mighty God, Everlasting Father, Prince of Peace.

You are a child of the King. You are the seed of
righteousness. On this day, we celebrate our heritage
as God's elect. I pray that today you are in great spirits.
I pray that you enjoy the fullness of God's presence
in your life. I pray that your heart is blessed by the
fellowship of friends and family. I praise God for his
son, our savior. I praise God that we know him!

_____

_____

_____

_____

_____

_____

I believe that God will restore what is broken in my life.

LAMENTATIONS 5:21 (NASB)
Restore us to You, O Lord, that we may be
restored; Renew our days as of old.

Our God is awesome and he specializes in fixing broken
things. God wants to come into your heart and your life
and fix the things that need mending. He loves you so
much. His heart beats for you. Invite him to that broken
place in your life. Trust in his restoration power!

I will prepare my heart, mind, and spirit to enter a new year.

1 PETER 1:3 (NIV)

Praise be to the God and Father of our Lord Jesus Christ! In his great mercy he has given us new birth into a living hope through the resurrection of Jesus Christ from the dead.

As we are just days away from a new year, I challenge you to reflect on the things you have experienced in the past 360 days. What things did you accomplish this year? What things changed in your life? Let this time of reflection serve as a guide for the things you want to accomplish next year. I pray that you continue to grow in the Lord and increase your hunger and thirst for his word. I also pray that you fully realize how amazing you are and how much God loves you!

DECEMBER 28

I will believe God for improvement
and increase in the new year.

REVELATION 21:5
He who was seated on the throne said, "I am
making everything new!" Then he said, "Write this
down, for these words are trustworthy and true.

God adores you. He loves to see you smile and he loves
when you look to him for guidance. He sees your efforts
and he knows your heart. He is so ready to propel you
into this next year, which will be an excellent year for
you! You will improve and increase in every area of
your life in the coming year. Walk confidently in this!

DECEMBER 29

I will have a vision board session with my family.

1 JOHN 3:22 (ESV)
And whatever we ask we receive from him, because we keep his commandments and do what pleases him.

A vision board is an excellent way to motivate and inspire you to keep moving toward your goals. It is a visual representation of things that you want to accomplish. It is the perfect activity to complete with your family. All you will need is a large board (big enough to be visible when hanging from your bedroom wall or another designated wall in your home), magazines, scissors, glue, tape, or tacks. You can search for magazine images that inspire and motivate you, or print pictures. Once you've found the pictures you want, use the adhesive of your choice to put them on your board. Once your board is complete, hang it where you will see it every day, preferably several times per day. Make this into a fun activity with your family!

DECEMBER 30

I will make paradigm changes instead
of New Year's resolutions.

EPHESIANS 4:22-24 (ESV)
To put off your old self, which belongs to your former
manner of life and is corrupt through deceitful desires,
and to be renewed in the spirit of your minds, and
to put on the new self, created after the likeness
of God in true righteousness and holiness.

It's that time of year again! In this season, people resolve
to lose weight, give up coffee or candy, or rid of some other
bad habit that they have tried to kick all year long. Although
there is nothing wrong with making plans to be a better
you, resolutions usually don't stick unless there is a shift in
behavior. What paradigm will you change in your life today?

_____

_____

_____

_____

_____

_____

I will no longer lack self-confidence. I am AFFIRMED.

PSALM 8:5
You have made them a little lower than the angels
and crowned them with glory and honor.

God is deeply and truly in love with you. When he created
you in his image, he said you are good. He said you are
intelligent. He said you are beautiful. He said you are
courageous. Most importantly, he said you are his!

_____

_____

_____

_____

_____

_____

_____

_____

_____

I pray that the daily quotes throughout this book have reassured you of exactly who you are in Christ. You will do amazing things this year, and I know that God has mind-blowing things in store for you! There is no goal too big and no dream too grand for God! May you always be encouraged, uplifted, and AFFIRMED!

Sources

About the Author

Nationally acclaimed bestselling author, transformational speaker, and success coach Cheryl Polote-Williamson has established multiple platforms, dedicating her consulting practice to cultivate innovative business solutions, strategic marketing initiatives, and financial acumen for entrepreneurs. A global leader, Cheryl is the CEO and founder of Williamson Media Group, LLC, and Cheryl Polote-Williamson, LLC, where her knowledge and expertise is used as a conduit to affirm others in pursuit of their purpose.

Cheryl's unmatched credibility in the industry has earned her numerous awards, including the Chocolate Social Award for best online community, the Dallas Top 25 Award, and the Female Success Factor Award. She has been named amongst the Who's Who In Black Dallas Publishing, held a position on the Forbes Coaches Council, and participates in the NAACP Author Pavilion, the Congressional Black Caucus, Christian Women in Media, and the National Association of Women Business Owners.

A prolific author and winner of the 2017 Indie Author Legacy Awards, Cheryl has published multiple books, including *Soul Reborn*, *Words from the Spirit for the 289 Spirit*, *Safe House*, *Affirmed*, *Soul Talk*, *Soul Bearer*, and *Soul Source*, with more titles on the way. She is also producing a play entitled *Soul Purpose*, set for a 2018 debut.

Cheryl and her husband, Russell, currently reside in Flower Mound, Texas. They have three beautiful children, Russell Jr., Lauren, and Courtney, as well as an adorable granddaughter, Leah. In her spare time, Cheryl enjoys traveling, reading, serving others, and spending quality time with family and friends.

To learn more, visit her website at
www.cherylpwilliamson.com

CREATING DISTINCTIVE BOOKS
WITH INTENTIONAL RESULTS

We're a collaborative group of creative masterminds
with a mission to produce high-quality books to position
you for monumental success in the marketplace.

Our professional team of writers, editors, designers,
and marketing strategists work closely together to ensure
that every detail of your book is a clear representation
of the message in your writing.

Want to know more?
Write to us at info@publishyourgift.com
or call (888) 949-6228

Discover great books, exclusive offers, and more at
www.PublishYourGift.com

Connect with us on social media

@publishyourgift

CPSIA information can be obtained
at www.ICGtesting.com
Printed in the USA
FSHW020207050120